The GOOD Hand Of GOD

One Man's Journey Into
The Realm Of The Supernatural

The GOOD Hand Of GOD

One Man's Journey Into The Realm Of The Supernatural

Bill Moody

Dawn Treader Publications
He who treads the dawn is the Bright and Shining Morning Star™

A Ministry of Morning Star And Company, Inc.
Cleveland, Pittsburgh, Detroit

THE GOOD HAND OF GOD
One Man's Journey into the Realm of the Supernatural

Published by Dawn Treader Publications
A ministry of Morning Star And Company, Inc.

Copyright © 2017 Bill Moody
All rights reserved. No part of this book may be reproduced or transmitted in any form or by any electronic or mechanical means, including information storage and retrieval systems, without the prior written permission of the publisher, except for brief quotations in printed reviews by reviewers.

Unless otherwise indicated, Scripture quotations used in this book are from The King James Version of the Bible (KJV) and The Holy Bible, New King James Version (NKJV). Copyright © 1982 Thomas Nelson Publishers, Nashville. Used by permission of Thomas Nelson Publishers. Throughout the write of this book there is no acknowledgement given to satan; wherever the name appears it is in lowercase.

For complete information:
Visit our Web site at www.dawntreaderpublications.com
Post Office Box 24405
Lyndhurst, Ohio 44124

Printed in the United States of America
First Edition: 2017
10 9 8 7 6 5 4 3 2 1
This title is also available as an ebook through Amazon Kindle.

Library Of Congress Cataloging-In-Publication Data

Names: Moody, Bill, 1946- author.
Title: The good hand of God : one man's journey into the realm of the supernatural / Bill Moody.
Description: First American Paperback Edition. | Cleveland Heights : Dawn Treader Publications, 2017. | Includes bibliographical references and index.
Identifiers: LCCN 2016008892 (print) | LCCN 2016011929 (ebook) | ISBN 9781589931251 (pbk. : alk. paper) | ISBN 9781589931268 (e-book : alk. paper) | ISBN 9781589931268 (e-book)
Subjects: LCSH: Presence of God. | Supernatural.
Classification: LCC BT180.P6 M66 2017 (print) | LCC BT180.P6 (ebook) | DDC 248--dc23
LC record available at http://lccn.loc.gov/2016008892

My thanks to Dr. Paul Edwards for his consultation and editorial work in the preparation of this manuscript. I also wish to thank Dr. Judy Byers and Dr. George Byers for their assistance with this project. A special thanks goes to my loving wife, Nancy for her enduring love and editorial support. Finally, I would like to thank my three wonderful children, Alethea, Kirsten and Kris for their constant encouragement.

Contents

Foreword   *i*
Introduction   *iii*

Light at the End of the Tunnel	1
Born Again	7
First Visible Manifestation	13
The Call to Preach	19
Shekinah Glory	25
The Out of Body Experience	31
The Holy Ghost in the Hall	37
The Dreams or Dreamer	43
The Vision	49
God Heals My Mother	55
Attacked by Devils	61
Voices, Voices, Voices	69
Jesus' Tomb	75
Manifestations of the Holy Ghost	83
The Miracle of Anna Lee	89
Manifestations and a Miracle	93
Streaks of His Presence	99
Just Like Him	105
Smoke, Fire, Oil, and Wings	111
Jesus Appears to Me	117
Heat, Wind, and Jesus	123
God in the Hands of Man	129
The Holy Ghost Like a Dove	135
The Miracle of the Oil	141
Face to Face	145
Epilogue	153

Foreword

While secularism abounds, most of us are striving for spiritual nourishment, consciously or unconsciously. For many, God is reduced to our unconscious and prayer to a passing conversation. The Good Hand of God provides a personal experience of the reality of God. This is not a book "about" God, but the direct experience of the presence of the living God. Bill Moody recounts for us his experiences of the divine presence of the Holy Spirit. The Good Hand of God is an inspiration to those too timid to open their lives to the presence and power of God's spirit in their lives.

Bill Moody is an inspired prophetic messenger of God. We can be grateful for this forthright treatment of a subject that many Christians too often have reduced to the level of banality. It is a testimony to the ecstasy of directly experiencing the radiance and rapture of the divine presence. Bill Moody's story of his personal relationship with God is like finding a long-buried treasure.

My earliest recollection of Bill Moody, some forty years ago, was as a college basketball player. He had an unstoppable baseline jumpshot. I now know him as an authentic

God-centered, spirit-filled person. As a native West Virginian, Bill knows that mountains are sacred places; places of visions. He is what I would call an anointed prophetic spiritual truth teller. As Bill explains, when he hears the inward voice of God speaking to him, God says to him "repeat what you hear."

Most of us are unaware of what a disciplined spiritual life means. There is, of course, a long-standing mystical tradition of divine awareness through rapturous visions. St. John of the Cross comes to mind. Reverend Moody describes such encounters. "Then the Holy Ghost came and stood about one foot away from me. I was now looking at God, the Holy Ghost face to face ... God moved closer and closer to me until he walked directly into my body."

What one finds here are Pentecostal power of healing miracles, prophecy, heavenly visitations, visions, and mystical experiences.

I found The Good Hand of God exhilarating and inspirational. I recommend it to those who want to restore the awakening of the miraculous and divine presence to their lives.

Dr. Paul Edwards

Introduction

The supernatural realm is a sea of uncharted questions and an ocean of unfathomable answers. Very few people ever experience the supernatural or even know of anyone who has. However, the twenty-first century church has turned the supernatural of God into the natural.

The early church experienced miracles, healings, and other supernatural phenomena. They knew and believed that God was a supernatural God who performed supernatural acts. My ministry and life have been influenced by the supernatural. From my youth to my adulthood the supernatural has been a common occurrence.

Under the guidance and direction of the Holy Ghost, I started maintaining a daily journal in 1980. These journals contain hundreds of supernatural phenomena that have punctuated my life and ministry. I was inspired by the Holy Ghost to write a book about these supernatural experiences. When I first wrote my experiences the Holy Ghost gave me the title "Face to Face With God" then proceeded to give me chapter titles and what experiences to write about. The Holy Ghost then gave me the text directly from His lips. I used no source or resource material of any kind.

Many of these supernatural experiences are similar in nature but they are truly different.

In this new and updated edition, "The Good Hand of God, One Man's Journey into the Realm of the Supernatural" I have also included an update of my life in the supernatural in the Epilogue. Also each chapter ends with a sampling of questions for thought and group discussion.

It is my prayer that you will reap bountifully from reading this book. I hope that your eyes and spirit will be opened to the supernatural power of God that awaits you.

The GOOD Hand Of GOD

One Man's Journey Into
The Realm Of The Supernatural

CHAPTER 1

Light at the End of the Tunnel

And as it is appointed unto men once to die,
but after this the judgment
Hebrews 9:27

As a child lying upon my bed at night I would think about dying. I would think about how it would feel to be dead. I would lay there in complete silence, visualizing being dead. Many nights I could not even go to sleep. Dying can't be that horrible I would say to myself. But then many other thoughts would invade my soul. Thoughts of does it hurt? Where do we go when we die? Is it total blackness there? Will I meet anyone else in this other world? The thoughts of dying would become so intense I would begin to shake and I thought the entire room was shaking.

My mind at times would be engrossed to the point of hysteria. With all these thoughts going on in my mind, I would pull the blanket over my head. Now, I was safe from dying, at least for the moment. I thought in the confines of my room in my bed nothing can happen to me.

These thoughts of death persisted into adolescence. As a teenager after having acquired a driver's license, I was involved in an accident. I was not injured in the accident, but thoughts of dying in an accident often plagued me.

In high school a fellow classmate became very ill. Throughout high school Paul was a perfect specimen of health, a weight lifter and football player. When he was diagnosed with leukemia, it sent shock waves through the entire senior class. How could he have leukemia? Paul stood five feet ten inches tall and weighed two hundred and twenty pounds. He clearly was the biggest, fastest, strongest and healthiest person on the football team. I knew if the doctors could not cure Paul he was going to die. This became a reoccurring thought on a daily basis and brought back all the emotions I once experienced.

Before bed each night I would wonder if Paul was going to die? If he died where would he go? Would he meet God or the devil? Many days I thought of Paul and what he must be thinking. Was he contemplating the things I wrestled with in my bed years ago? I envisioned how he was coping with the surety that in a matter of months he would be dead? How would he deal with death, the greatest negative force in the universe?

My classmates and I looked deep within our souls for answers but we found none. We imagined it could be one of us instead of Paul. In twelve months time he became a mere shadow of his former self. I would often visit him, and I watched him rapidly deteriorate.

When Paul died six months later on a cloudy Wednesday morning my questions about death were still unanswered. I could only imagine how it felt. Did it hurt? Where did he go and who did he see? As he lay there in the casket not moving, eyes closed, my mind took me back to happier times of football, basketball and the Junior Prom that we shared together. Paul was buried and we went our separate ways, but I never forgot him.

I enrolled at Fairmont State College in 1964 and joined

the basketball team. The next two years playing basketball proved to be very exciting and rewarding. In my junior year I excelled and became the team's leading scorer. In January 1968 while playing West Liberty State College, I scored 18 of our teams 22 points in 12 minutes. Then tragedy struck as I drove to the basket to score a lay up. An opposing player landed on my back, and I came down on my left knee. I heard something pop. I had torn the cartilage and ligaments in my left knee. I watched my knee swell to the size of a ripe cantaloupe and my life time dream evaporate.

I was unable to relinquish my career completely. I managed to regain some of my ability after surgery while wearing a knee brace. However, my movement was hampered. I could only run in a straight line and my self-confidence was not there. Unable to regain my old form, I became very depressed and suicidal. I also cultivated a penchant for women other than my future wife, Nancy.

In March I had a scheduled doctor's appointment with my orthopedic surgeon. I had been suffering from flu like symptoms for several days and was running a low-grade fever. My appointment was scheduled for 11:00 a.m. Thursday, and since I was not feeling well my father volunteered to ride with me to Pittsburgh.

My father and I discussed my knee injury and what further treatment it may or may not entail. We arrived in Pittsburgh and after ten minutes of waiting the doctor appeared. My father and I followed him into the examination room. The doctor examined my left knee. After a brief examination he said, my knee was in excellent condition and for me to continue with rehabilitation. He also informed me that he was going to give me a cortisone injection. After he gave me the injection he had me to lie there for about twenty minutes. He explained that some people have an adverse reaction to a cortisone injection. So I had to relax for a little while.

I lay on the examination table for about twenty minutes when the nurse came in and informed me I could leave. As we started down the hall to the elevators, I told my father I did not feel very well. After a couple more steps, I turned to my father and said to him, "I think I'm going to pass out." Then immediately I fell unconscious to the floor. The last thing I remembered was everything going black. I don't even recall hitting the floor. As I lay unconscious, thoughts of death emerged. I asked myself, "am I dead? If I am dead this feels great." I remember years before asking, "How does it feel to die?"

I found myself standing in a long tunnel and on both sides of the tunnel was a long row of lights. Just ahead of me was a very bright light. I started to move toward the very large bright light at the end of the tunnel. I noticed that I wasn't walking but being carried along as if drawn by a magnet to the very bright light. Half way down this tunnel, as I approached this very bright light, I was drawn backward. But I did not want to leave the light at the end of the tunnel. I was being drawn back, back to the beginning of the tunnel where I regained consciousness. My father, doctors and nurses stood over me as I lay there on the hospital floor. Thoughts still rang in my mind that I did not want to leave the bright warm light at the end of the tunnel. After a few minutes I sat up and eventually stood on my feet as we departed the hospital.

On the drive back to Fairmont all I could think about was that light at the end of the tunnel. My thoughts were death is not bad after all because there's light at the end of the tunnel.

Death is the greatest negative force in the universe and should not be a topic that we should be afraid of, ignore, or put into the back of our minds. Death is inevitable. We will all die; it's just a matter of when. The most important thing about death is that it opens a door to another life. Whether you are young or old death will come knocking at your door one day. It doesn't matter whether you welcome it or not. Death is not going to leave without you when your turn comes. The Apostle Paul said, "It's appointed unto man once to die, but after that the judgment" (Hebrews 9:27).

Jesus was the light at the end of the tunnel. Death is just a new door that opens up to Jesus who is the life giving door. For me, Jesus was waiting at the end of the tunnel to take me into eternity. But Jesus was not ready for me because it was not my time to be with him. When my time comes I know Jesus will be there to greet me into the halls of heaven.

Questions for Group Discussion:

1. How often do you think about dying?
2. Do you look into your fears, thoughts, and feelings about death?
3. Where do you believe you will spend eternity?

CHAPTER

Born Again

*Most assuredly, I say to you, unless one is born again,
he cannot see the kingdom of God.*
John 3:3

As a youngster growing up in Grant Town, West Virginia in the early 1950's I never really thought about God much. My mother talked about God and said that one should go to church on a regular basis. Although my mother believed in God, she did not go to church herself, and I wondered why. She would often say to me, "I don't want to go to church and be a hypocrite like some other people I know." In her always in-charge voice she would make that statement and I would always listen with interest.

Looking back my mother was correct about the hypocrisy. As a young boy I witnessed a lot of unchristian behavior. Often I witnessed lying, stealing, adultery, fornication, lasciviousness, witchcraft, strife, drunkenness, revellings and the like. Many of those so-called church people played cards, gambled and even played numbers.

We had a Baptist and Methodist church that was separated by 100 yards of open field. As I grew older mother started sending my oldest sister, Zinola, and me to church. I thought it was fun. I would meet all my neighborhood friends there, especially a few girls that I was always fond of but too shy to approach.

Those people, "hypocrites" as mother called them, would frequent the local bars on Saturday night and be in church on Sunday morning. Everybody knew that a particular married man was having an adulterous affair with a married woman. It appeared that everybody in town was involved in some unchristian amorous activity. You could often see people late at night lurking and hiding in the shadows waiting for a rendezvous with a lover.

Grant Town was a coal mining town and many of the town residents were employed by the coal mines. The mines claimed many lives. On Sunday mornings Sunday School and church for the most part were full. Often if you did not come early you could not find a good seat. My sister and I always arrived early so I could sit beside a few girls I liked.

Deacon James Dean was one of the Sunday School teachers who taught us every Sunday morning. I really enjoyed the class because it was very interesting and informative. I also liked having a chance to interact in class. Morning worship service was eventful enough, but it wasn't as exciting as Sunday School. The choirs would sing and we sang along in the congregation, but the songs did not mean that much to me. The Pastor, William Roper, would pray and run the entire morning service with vigor.

There would be frequent shouts from the choir and congregation saying, "Amen Pastor." Many times some of the people would faint, cry, and would even stand, saying things like, "You're preaching now!" Often Reverend Roper would preach, shout, and moan. Sometimes I could understand him and sometimes I could not. More often than not I would put my head down and laugh with the other youngsters in the congregation. At times we pretended to be preaching as the pastor did, mocking and mimicking his every move. Whenever he would moan or groan, we would moan and groan then start laughing very quietly. Reverend Roper would preach so hard he began to sweat. He would then take a handkerchief from the pulpit and wipe his forehead. This did not go unnoticed by the youngsters in the congregation, as we also pretended to have handkerchiefs and wipe the sweat from our brows and foreheads.

One Sunday morning Reverend Roper preached from the Gospel according to Saint John. Jesus spoke to Nicodemus and told him, "Ye must be born again . . . " (John 3:3). For years those words were forever written upon the fleshy tablets of my heart. I really had no idea, just as Nicodemus, what those words really meant until many years later. I continued to attend church as a youngster and even until high school. Then I stopped going. Basketball and football had replaced church and its functions and activities. The excitement of church was surpassed by the excitement of sports and teenage girls. I would, on occasion, special occasions, return to church, but for the most part church had become boring and out of date for me.

In 1976 my wife, Nancy, and I were living on Spruce Street in Fairmont. We had a daughter named Alethea. Life as a rule was a series of ups and downs for us; our marriage was in trouble coupled with financial woes. I had been smoking, drinking and dating other women for a few years. My job gave me no satisfaction and I had many thoughts of committing suicide. I would drive my car down Interstate 79 South and try to talk myself into crossing the median strip into an oncoming tractor trailer.

At this time I was attending Mount Zion Baptist Church every Sunday morning. My life was so horrible that I did not know where to turn to get help. I began reading the Bible and a book by Kenneth Hagin called "New Thresholds of Faith." I tried to stop smoking, but I could not. Many nights I would rip up an entire pack of cigarettes and throw them into the trash. The next morning the craving for a cigarette would be so strong I would go through the trash, find a broken cigarette, and smoke it.

This continued for six months. It was torture, and my addiction to cigarettes would not go away. One night as I lay upon my bed sleeping, I had a dream that seemed very real. The picture of Jesus that I had stolen in 1964 hung at the foot of our bed on the wall. In this dream I could see Jesus come out of the picture in a counter clock wise motion and stand before me about five feet away. I was on my knees asking Jesus to come closer, but He refused to do so. Jesus was just standing there and appeared to be floating in mid-air. I had my eyes fixed on Him. This went on for quite some time then suddenly from my right appeared a pack of cigarettes moving very slowly to my left. With my right hand I pushed the pack of cigarettes out of the dream. Since the cigarettes were no longer in the vision of the dream, Jesus immediately came closer. Jesus came, stood directly in front of me about a foot away, and smiled at me with the most beautiful smile I had ever seen. The next morning all I could remember was Jesus standing in front of me with that beautiful smile.

I recounted the dream over and over again in my mind

as to the meaning of Jesus appearing to me. I continued to smoke but had a deep desire to stop which seemed to grow in intensity daily. Two weeks later while reading the Bible along with Hagin's book, I decided to have a bowl of cereal. I walked into the kitchen with a cigarette in my hand. I placed the cigarette in the ashtray on the kitchen table and took a bowl out of the cabinet. Then I went to the cupboard, picked up the box of corn flakes and poured out a bowl full. I added sugar and milk from the refrigerator and poured some on the cereal. As I placed the milk back in the refrigerator, picked up the cigarette to smoke it, a hand grabbed mine. I tried with all my strength to put the cigarette to my mouth, but this hand held my hand so I could not. Then with great force this hand, which held mine, put out the cigarette in the ash tray. I was amazed and startled. After an hour of praise and worship, deep reflection, meditation and somberness I was able to finish the cereal.

Later, after reading the Bible I got on my knees to pray. I asked the Lord Jesus to "sanctify and justify me." As I was on my knees in the living room in front of the couch, the power of God seemed to fill the room. Then all of a sudden a hand grabbed my head, pushed it into the front of the couch, burying it. I began to cry. Unable to stop crying, I stood to my feet with hands raised toward heaven. I saw angels moving around the room, and heavenly music filled the room. I looked down at the floor; it appeared as if I was off the ground about six inches. I could not feel my feet on the floor anymore. I tried to touch the floor, but could not reach it. This lasted for ten minutes, but seemed like it went on for an hour or more. I never heard such singing and music before in my entire life. I knew I was truly changed that night.

Thoughts returned of Reverend William Roper and Jesus as He said, "Ye must be born again." From that night on I never smoked another cigarette, drank, or said a foul word. That night in my living room I knew in my heart that God, the Holy Ghost, had visited me. I can truly say that as Jesus spoke to Nicodemus, "Ye must be born again," I, too, had a born again experience.

QUESTIONS FOR GROUP DISCUSSION:

1. Discuss your church experiences and the impact they have had on your life.
2. Have you been born again?
3. Describe your born again experience.

CHAPTER

First Visible Manifestation

*For the Spirit searches all things,
yes, the deep things of God.*
1 Corinthians 2:10

While attending church as a youngster, I would often hear the preacher mention the words Holy Ghost. He would say things like, "You need the Holy Ghost" or, "Get filled with the Holy Ghost." My Sunday school teacher would often talk about the Holy Ghost. I was still puzzled about this Holy Ghost. For many years I heard many people talk about the Holy Ghost, but I still did not quite understand. To say the least I was quite ignorant about the Holy Ghost and His work in the Godhead.

My first visible manifestation of the Holy Ghost was stupendous. I remember it as if it only happened yesterday. Words cannot adequately describe the unbelievable things that transpired that day. Let me explain some things about the Holy Ghost which will greatly enhance my first visible manifestation of Him. It will give us insight into His work and purpose.

My mother, Rose Lee Moody, was born with a veil over her face, which in reality was a small piece of skin over her eyes. She attributes this to her ability to be able, as she calls it, "to see things" in the supernatural. In fact it is the Holy Ghost that lets her see and dream the things that she sees.

First, let's answer the question "Who is the Holy Ghost?" We can answer the question by asking two more questions. Is the Holy Ghost really God? Is the Holy Ghost really a person? To reiterate, the Holy Ghost is not a force, wind, it, what or will-o'-the-wisp and smoky presence coming from God. In many churches for years the Holy Ghost was thought of as some influence or unknown force, something we could get our hands on to use. Just the very opposite is true. He is a Person who gets hold of us and uses us. It is a matter of the Holy Ghost having power, He is striving to use us for the greater glory of God. The Holy Ghost is not a what, but one third of the Godhead. So the question is not "what is the Holy Ghost, but who is the Holy Ghost?" The Godhead also known as the Holy Trinity consists of God the Father, God the Son (Jesus Christ) and God the Holy Ghost. Many people today are very ignorant about the Holy Ghost in the Bible just as I was as a youngster. Many Christians simply are unaware of the person and work of the Holy Ghost.

In many churches today across America I have witnessed the insufficiency of the presence and power of the Holy Ghost. The problem is that many have a doctrine or theology of a presence without a really true presence. Many talk about the Holy Ghost as if He is some force that blows in and out church services. The Holy Ghost, in many churches, has been replaced by humans who want to take over the reins of power and presence. To state it another way, the Holy Ghost has been replaced by church machinery and church programs. What we have in Christendom today is a Holy Ghostless Christianity. We need more people who believe in the Holy Ghost in our denominational churches. Thousands of Christians are in the dark when it comes to matters of the Holy Ghost. Many professed Christian believers are dominated by thoughts of self and success. Many so-called Christians truly believe in the Holy Ghost, just as long as He acts properly and blesses their activities without His help.

Many Christians are running from or denying the presence and power of the Holy Ghost. If we would concentrate on letting Him take control of our lives we would be stronger spiritually. The most important thing to remember is that you do not use the Holy Ghost; the Holy Ghost uses you. The Holy Ghost wants to possess you because your body is the temple of the Holy Ghost. What you believe or think about the Holy Ghost can and will determine your spiritual awareness. What you believe is extremely important. The church is in utter turmoil today because of wrong denominational beliefs about the Holy Ghost.

The Holy Ghost is God. The holy scriptures pronounce that the Holy Ghost is God. In Isaiah 61:1 the Holy Ghost is spoken of as the Lord God. The Holy Ghost was speaking through the Prophet Isaiah and made that pronouncement. Jesus Himself proclaims that the Holy Ghost which is the Comforter is truly God (John 14:16). Throughout the holy scriptures the Holy Ghost is equal with God. The Holy Ghost is equal in person, position and responsibility with the Father and the Son (Matthew 28:19).

The Holy Ghost is a Spirit person that has divine characteristics known as attributes. The Holy Ghosts is eternal. He is described as the "the eternal Spirit" (Hebrews 9:14). The Bible says that the Holy Ghost is everywhere present. He is described as having omnipresence (Psalm 139:7-10). He is all powerful as mentioned in Luke 1:35 as "the Power of the Highest shall overshadow thee." Finally, the Holy Ghost is said to be all knowing or omniscient "for the Spirit searcheth all things, yea, the deep things of God" (1 Corinthians 2:10). The works of the Holy Ghost declare His deity. We can see His works in many places in scripture as mentioned in the following: In the creation (Genesis 1:2), inspiration (2 Timothy 3:16), regeneration (Titus 3:5), conversion (John 16:8-11), baptism (1 Corinthians 12:13), sealing (Ephesians 4:30) and sanctification (Galatians 5:22, 23).

As the President of the United States is the top executive officer in this country, the Holy Ghost is the great executor in the Godhead plan. The Holy Ghost works on all levels, planes and spheres. With having this background or backdrop of the Holy Ghost now firmly implanted in our spirits let us look at my first visible manifestation.

At the time of my first visible manifestation of the Holy Ghost, I was living in Fairmont. I had just been delivered from cigarette smoking and experienced an incredible born again experience. It was 1976 and some months had elapsed. Two weeks prior to this great manifestation of the Holy Ghost I appeared on station WLYJ Christian Television and gave my testimony of how God had saved me and delivered me from cigarettes.

A viewer had watched me give my testimony and wrote me a letter. I was in the kitchen sitting at the table writing a letter in response. I was about half way through this letter. No one was in the house with me. It was very quiet. The telephone had not rang all day. As I sat there in the chair I felt the overpowering presence of God fill the kitchen and the downstairs living room. I continued to write the letter as the presence of God grew greater and greater. It reached a point that the presence of God was so strong that I felt something more going on other than just His presence. The moment that the presence of God reached its highest point, I no longer could continue to write. I felt an overwhelming presence of God over my right shoulder at the kitchen table. At first I was very reluctant to glance over my right shoulder. What or who could it be standing over my right shoulder? All I knew was that something or somebody had invaded my kitchen and living room. I waited a few moments, and then turned my head around. I saw a man standing about six feet tall and glowing.

This man had a body, but it was not a flesh and blood body rather a spirit body. He had hands, feet that did not have shoes on them, and was dressed in a robe. He had a body that you could not see through. As I was looking at this man, his presence grew in intensity and power. He stood behind me for about 20 seconds. He was looking at me, and I was staring in great wonder at him. My thoughts were "is this Jesus, is this an Angel or is this God?" Then, as I was staring at this person, he slowly disappeared. What in the world had I experienced. I knew something supernatural had taken place. Had I not been a rational person, my thoughts of the experience would have driven me to a point of disbelief. Looking back at that experience today, as supernatural as it was in every respect, I know it was God.

I know what I saw that day in my kitchen was truly God the Holy Ghost. This first visible manifestation of the Holy Ghost was an amazing experience. Unknown to me at that time was that I was to experience many more visible manifestations of the Holy Ghost.

Questions for Group Discussion:

1. How is it possible for the Holy Ghost, the Comforter, to be equal with God?
2. Have you ever seen an angel or Jesus? Were you fearful or at peace?

CHAPTER

The Call to Preach

Lord, what do You want me to do?
Acts 9:6

When I was young I often thought why does a person become a minister? How does he do it? Does he go to school or does a church call him? I asked those questions every time I saw a minister on television.

As I got older I saw that there were quite a few ministers. I later realized that there were thousands and possibly millions of ministers across the country. But this still did not answer my questions. How does a person become a minister?

Along the way I learned you could attend a Bible college or a theological seminary. Was this the way? Did one have to go to a seminary or was there another method? Sometimes I would listen in amazement how these ministers could speak for hours about the Bible. Many of them could quote scripture one right after the other without stopping.

There were many styles of preaching that I witnessed over the years. Some would quietly speak putting forth some biblical views to make a desired point while others would scream, yell, and even moan as they were preaching.

Through asking many questions of many people I discovered each man or woman's style of preaching was different. While talking with Reverend James Jackson he told me, "People are called or chosen by God for the ministry." I proceeded to ask him, "does God speak to a person when He calls him or her?" Reverend Jackson's response was, "God speaks to men all the time." Being young and immature I could not understand how God spoke to people.

The Bible gave some examples of God calling individuals into the ministry. In the Old Testament the most dramatic call into the ministry was that of Moses.

One day while he was tending the flock of Jethro, his father-in-law the priest of Midian, Moses led the flock to the backside of the desert where he came to the mountain of God which was called Horeb. While Moses was at the base of Horeb the Angel of the Lord appeared to him. The most astounding thing about this appearance of God was that He appeared in a flame of fire out of a bush. Amazed Moses turned aside to see this great sight. God had heard the cries and seen the afflictions of His people from heaven. Now He had come down to deliver His people from the Egyptians. God had come down to give them a large, good land flowing with milk and honey. God called Moses into the ministry to be the deliverer of His people (Exodus 3). Moses accepted his call into the ministry to be God's man to deliver the nation of Israel from its oppressors.

In the New Testament there is another spectacular calling into the ministry. That was the call of the Apostle Paul. In the third chapter of Philippians the Apostle Paul gives an early account of himself. Paul said he was circumcised the eighth day, the stock of Israel, from the tribe of Benjamin, a Hebrew. He continued to state that he was a pharisee, zealous in persecuting the church. The pharisees were a sect of self-righteous and zealous Jews who held to the letter of the Law. Saint Luke gives us an account of the Apostle Paul's amazing call into the ministry (Acts 9).

Paul had acquired letters from the high priest to go to Damascus to the synagogues. If Paul would find any believers in Christ whether male or female, he would bring them bound to Jerusalem. Paul began his journey and as he came close to Damascus suddenly a bright light from heaven was shining about him. Paul fell from his horse to the ground where he heard the voice of Jesus. When Paul rose from the ground he was blind. He was then taken to Damascus. After three days without food and water, Paul was healed and filled with the Holy Ghost. He received his sight and after eating he was strengthened. Straightway he began preaching Christ in the synagogues.

All through the Bible God has come to men in dreams and revealed His will to them. Miriam and Aaron complained against Moses because he married an Ethiopian woman. They also spoke against Moses because God made him the deliverer of Israel. God heard the conversation among the three and proceeded to tell them how He visits men. God Almighty came down in a pillar of a cloud and stood in the door of the tabernacle. Good spoke to Moses, Aaron and Miriam and said, "Hear now my words: If there be a prophet among you, I the Lord will make myself known unto him in a vision and will speak unto him in a dream" (Numbers 12).

My own call into the ministry was also supernatural. Jesus came to me first in a dream. My call into the ministry was received in a dream. In the spring of 1978 I would read the Bible before bed and then pray. I retired for the night and almost immediately I was asleep.

In this early morning dream I was sitting on a fallen tree in the midst of a lot of other trees. Directly in front of me was a large open field about one hundred yards wide and one hundred yards long. As I sat there on this fallen tree dressed in what appeared to be a gray garment, a man who I did not recognize appeared from the left with a yoke of oxen and a plow. As the plow was tilling the soil, the man walking behind the plow was dropping seeds into the ground. He continued to drop seeds into the soil for about fifty yards. Then this man turned and walked toward me. He was dressed completely in a white robe down to his feet. He was carrying a brown bag of seeds which he opened when he reached me. I looked into the bag and he said to "put some whitener in it." Then he turned, walked away and started tilling the soil again dropping seeds as he did before.

When I looked into the bag I saw the most amazing thing. The seeds were moving as if they were alive. The man looked like Jesus although he did not say he was Jesus. I awakened from this dream. For weeks I tried to understand what it all meant especially when he said "put some whitener in it." I was astonished at the bag of seeds that were moving as if alive. A number of months passed after receiving this dream. I talked to many ministers about what it all meant. I was told that God was calling me into the ministry, and I later realized that the seeds were the Word of God.

Months later as I was driving from Clarksburg, West Virginia, the Holy Ghost spoke to me saying, "I want you to do it." At first I did not understand what was happening to me. This voice came from the passenger seat of the car as if someone were sitting there. Then the Holy Ghost spoke again and he said, "I want you to preach." About this time I was crying profusely. I was in tears, and could barely see to drive. The Holy Ghost, God, had just spoken to me and called me into the ministry.

Weeks after this experience I went over it hundreds of times knowing that God Himself had called me into the ministry. The voice that I heard in the car with me that evening changed my life forever.

Questions for Group Discussion:

1. Have you ever heard God speak to you? What did it sound like?
2. How can one be certain that he or she has been called into the ministry?
3. Discuss the similarities and differences between Moses and Paul's call by God.

CHAPTER

Shekinah Glory

The sight of the glory of the Lord was like
a consuming fire on the top of the mountain
Exodus 24:17

The prophet and deliverer, Moses, was privileged in that he saw the Shekinah glory of God. Scripture says, "And the glory of the Lord abode upon Mount Sinai and the cloud covered it six days: and the seventh day he called unto Moses out of the midst of the cloud" (Exodus 24:16). Moses had ascended Mount Sinai for the sixth time. He describes what he saw when arriving at the apex of the mountain. In Moses' eyes the glory of the Lord appeared as a cloud that covered the entire mountain. On the seventh day having been called by God out of the midst of the cloud, Moses came forth. Moses describes what he saw "And the sight of the glory of the Lord was like devouring fire on the top of the mount in the eyes of the children of Israel" (Exodus 24:17). Moses describes God's glory as seen with human eyes like a consuming fire.

Gazing upon the Shekinah glory of God was one of the greatest honors that could be placed upon any man. Moses was a special man with a special mission that God needed him to perform. This would not be the last time that he would see the Shekinah Gory of God.

In Solomon's dedication of the temple we read of the manifestation of the Shekinah glory. Once the temple had been completed, Solomon assembled the elders, tribal heads in Jerusalem. He wanted them to bring up the Ark of the Covenant of the Lord out of Zion. With all the elders of Israel present and the priests, the Levites brought up the Ark of the Lord, and the tabernacle of meeting. They also brought all the holy vessels that were in the tabernacle. King Solomon and all the congregation of Israel offered untold multitude of sacrifices before the Ark. Then the priests brought in the Ark of the Covenant of the Lord into the inner sanctuary under the outstretched wings of the cherubim.

The priests had been arranging the furniture and taking care of what was necessary; then they left. Suddenly something amazing happened in the temple. The presence of God entered the holy place in the form of a cloud. The Shekinah glory of God filled the entire temple. Scripture says, "And it came to pass, when the priests were come out of the holy place, that the cloud filled the house of the Lord," (1 Kings 8:10). "So that the priests could not stand to minister because of the cloud: for the glory of the Lord had filled the house of the Lord" (1 Kings 8:11). What a tremendous act of God's majesty and omnipotence displayed at the dedication of God's temple.

The great prophet Isaiah described the Shekinah glory of God in meticulous detail. The prophet said he saw the Lord sitting upon a throne, and He was high and lifted up. Imagine the God of the whole earth appearing to the prophet Isaiah and imagine what was going on inside his head. Isaiah said that the train of God filled the entire temple. He says, "In the year that King Uzziah died I saw also the Lord sitting upon a throne, high and lifted up, and his train filled the temple" (Isaiah 6:1). Isaiah was just one of many who actually saw God in bodily form. Isaiah said he saw God in the temple and although not stated directly it was probably Solomon's temple. More than likely Isaiah was in the Holy of Holies when the Shekinah glory appeared to him.

Isaiah says, "and one cried unto another and said, holy, holy, holy, is the Lord of hosts: the whole world is full of His glory" (Isaiah 6:3). Isaiah says the Shekinah glory of God filled the entire earth with His presence. Isaiah continues in verse four, "and the posts of the door moved at the voice of him that cried and the house was filled with smoke." Notice that Isaiah said the Shekinah glory of God filled the temple and also that smoke accompanied Him. "...for mine eyes have seen the King, the Lord of Hosts:" (Isaiah 6:4). Isaiah, like most people in ancient times, felt superstitious that if one saw God he would die.

A man would naturally feel unclean, undone, and corrupt before the presence of God Almighty. Standing in the presence of God does not automatically carry a death sentence. Isaiah had seen the King, the Lord of Hosts and lived to talk about it. Even more importantly the King, the Lord of Hosts would speak with him.

In the Gospel according to Saint Luke we have another account of the Shekinah glory of God. Jesus had just been born in Bethlehem, and there came this great pronouncement from God. Luke gives this account in Luke 2:8, "And there were in the same country shepherds abiding in the field, keeping watch over their flock by night." There were a group of shepherds attending to their flocks when this great announcement came virtually from nowhere. "And, lo, the angel of the Lord came upon them, and the glory of Lord shone round about them: and they were sore afraid" (Luke 2:9). God the King, the Lord of Hosts appeared to the shepherds that night to give them the good news of Jesus' birth. The Shekinah glory of God always symbolized God's presence as seen in Exodus 24:16; 1 Kings 8:10; and Isaiah 6:1-3. The shepherds had seen and heard the Shekinah glory of God that night with the birth of Jesus.

My encounter with the Holy ghost on July 22, 1982 was of great importance and significance. This encounter would set in motion a chain reaction of manifestations that would come with great regularity. Within less than a month I would personally encounter the Shekiniah glory that Moses, King Solomon, Isaiah, and the shepherds had seen.

On August 9th the day started as any other day. The kids were off to school and I went to work. I came home from work and Nancy left for work and, as was the plan, I picked up the kids at the babysitter. I gave the kids their dinner and helped them with their homework. We all watched television for about an hour and then I put them to bed. I prayed some more, read the Bible and prepared to go pick up my wife. As I sat there on the bed I started putting on my shoes. I put the first shoe on and then I started to put on the second. Then all of a sudden as from nowhere a man, the Angel of Lord, appeared. He was about six feet tall and emanating from Him was a great bright light that shone all around Him. This light was so bright that it lit up the entire hallway and my bedroom. Kris was in bed behind me asleep, so who was it that went down the hall as a bright light? I started down the hallway and the majesty and glory of God had filled it. The glory of God was so thick in the hall one could literally feel and touch God. His presence permeated the entire carpet, walls, curtains, furniture and house. I could not at this point stand. I began to fall down as I walked into the kitchen. I was looking for this person that shone as the sun as He walked down the hall. In the kitchen, I held on to the kitchen table so I would not fall to the floor.

In the kitchen I first noticed this very thick blue smoke that covered the entire area. I made my way to the dining room and again I held on to the dining room table as this blue smoke became thicker. I could see this smoke -- it felt as if God, the Shekiniah glory, was touching me as I walked. As I entered the living room I could see that this blue smoke had now entirely filled the house. The Shekinah glory, the King, the Lord of Host was at my home with me. Now I could stand no longer as the Shekinah glory of God was so intense and powerful. I fell to my knees with uplifted hands trembling. I began to praise and worship Him. The presence of God's glory lasted about fifteen minutes as the smoke filled the entire house. I felt so unworthy, unclean and undone in His mighty presence. The presence of the Shekinah glory was so intense, majestic and powerful that I just wept hard. I have never in my life seen or felt anything that even came close to that manifestation of the Shekinah glory.

When I was able to stand again, the smoke began to disappear very slowly. As the smoke disappeared, the brightness that had made the house as light as the light of day disappeared. This had been without question the most stupendous experience I ever had. The Shekinah glory had come down from heaven as with Moses, King Solomon, Isaiah, and the shepherds. He had come down from heaven and visited me in a dramatic fashion and in a majestic manifestation of His Shekinah glory. My life changed dramatically after this visitation and profoundly changed my perception of God.

Questions for Group Discussion:

1. Are the terms Angel of the Lord, Shekinah glory, and God interchangeable?
2. Discuss the meaning of the cloud, the glory of the Lord, and a consuming fire as told in Exodus 24.

CHAPTER 6

The Out of Body Experience

Whether in the body I do not know,
or whether out of the body I do not know, God knows
2 Corinthians 12:2

The Apostle Paul had one of the most exciting experiences recorded in the Bible. He had experienced many things in many places that taught him to be humble, but this was one of the greatest. He describes it in his second letter to the church at Corinth this way, "I knew a man in Christ above fourteen years ago whether in the body, I cannot tell; or whether out of the body, I cannot tell; God knoweth such an one caught up to the third heaven" (2 Corinthians 12:2). Paul takes a moment to boast to answer his enemies at Corinth about visions and revelations (verse one). These revelations are the unveiling of things that were not known before which only God alone could make known to him.

This particular experience takes place about 46 A.D. some 14 years after Christ's crucifixion. Just where Paul saw it is not readily known. He explains he could have been in the body, as the case with Enoch, Elijah, and John (Genesis 5:24; 2 Kings 2; Revelations 4:1) or out of the body during this vision. He said he was caught up to the third heaven. He makes reference to being caught up in his letter to the church at Thessalonica. "Then we which are alive and remain shall be caught up together with them in the clouds, to meet the Lord in the air: and so shall we ever be with the Lord" (1 Thessalonians 4:17). Paul was not at all doubtful of being caught up to the third heaven. Of this he was very sure. The holy scriptures mention three heavens in context to what Paul has stated.

The first heaven is the clouds as stated in Genesis 1:8 and Psalms 77:17-18. The second is the starry space as found in Genesis 15:5; Deuteronomy 1:10; and Isaiah 13:10. The third heaven is the place or planet heaven as revealed in Genesis 1:1; Isaiah 14:12-14; and Revelation 21:2,10. Paul stated that he was caught up into paradise and heard unspeakable words. "How that he was caught up into paradise, and heard unspeakable words, which it is not lawful for a man to utter" (2 Corinthians 12:4).

This paradise of which he is speaking is in the third heaven where God resides. Paul says that he heard unspeakable words that were not lawful for a man to utter. It meant that human lips and tongue were not able to express them adequately. It might have been that they were too sacred to repeat to another human being. What an absolutely undescribable, unspeakable experience that must have been. This experience must have really changed Paul's entire life and ministry. Having been in the presence of God with all His glory and power gave Paul a great desire to spread the gospel.

The Apostle John was banished to the wind swept Greek isle of Patmos for his testimony of Jesus Christ. He experienced probably one of the greatest things that could ever happen to any one person. "After this I looked, and behold, a door was opened in heaven: and the first voice which I heard was as it were of a trumpet talking with me; which said, come up hither, and I will shew thee things which must be hereafter" (Revelation 4:1). John standing on earth looked into heaven where a door was opened. He heard a voice that sounded like a trumpet talking with him. The voice was that of Jesus. John said he was in the Spirit on the Lord's day, and heard behind me a great voice as of a trumpet" (Revelations 1:10). John was in the Spirit because he was entirely in union with the Holy Ghost and entirely surrendered to him. Then John made an incredible statement that he was in the spirit and a throne was set before him in heaven. This is the second time that he makes mention of being in the spirit. "And immediately I was in the spirit; and behold, a throne was set in heaven and one sat on the throne" (Revelations 4:2).

We see Jesus in verse one tell John to "come up hither" into heaven. The question becomes was he raptured, did he see a vision or was it an out of body experience? Was he taken into heaven in the flesh, and beheld a throne and saw one sitting on the throne? Maybe he saw a vision while in the spirit on the Lord's Day. It could have been that he actually had an out of body experience in the spirit. Jesus told him to come up hither of that we know that John obeyed and stood around the throne of God. As Paul was caught up into paradise whether in the body or out of the body he could not tell. One thing we do know is that these supernatural occurrences have been well documented. The Bible makes reference to them as well as personal accounts of Christians and others who have had similar experiences.

In 1981 and like Paul, as well as many others, I experienced an out of body experience. During this time of my life and ministry I spent hours in prayer, reading a great deal, and much of my time was devoted to fasting, memorizing scripture, and meditation. It was during this early part of my ministry that I read all kinds of Christian books. There was always a hunger and thirst for the supernatural of God. I would pray for hours a day at home and in the church for the supernatural to take place. I was never satisfied with just the ordinary in my Christian life. This hunger and thirst was an all consuming desire to experience Jesus Christ in the fullest. This desire to experience Jesus was a thirst that never seemed to be satisfied. My thoughts all day were to experience the Holy Ghost in greater spiritual depths. Fasting and prayer heightened my desire to seek God with all my soul and spirit daily. I so much wanted to experience the supernatural because the Bible is a supernatural book. But more importantly God is a supernatural God that operates in the realm of miracles.

The supernatural should not be the exception; the supernatural should be the rule. God is not supernatural some of the time; He is supernatural all of the time. This hunger and thirst for the supernatural had been realized by me in some measure in my ministry, but increasingly the manifestations of the Holy Ghost had become more frequent and pronounced. While at Welcome Baptist Church, Pastor James Jackson and I experienced great answers to prayer for the sick. Many were healed of diseases and all sorts of torments. It was in one of these Wednesday night prayer meetings that I experienced one of the greater manifestations of God.

This particular Wednesday night seemed no different from any other we had. We had a great service; then it was my turn to expound on some biblical truth. I stood to my feet and began to speak about God in the church. I continued speaking for about ten minutes when I felt the Holy Ghost all over my body. As I stood there speaking, my spirit moved right out of my body backwards. I could see myself, the body of flesh, dressed in a three piece brown suit. I saw the back of my head and back as I stood there in the spirit. I was out of my body. I could see the flesh body still talking and ministering to the congregation. My spirit body looked exactly like me in every respect. I looked down at my hands. They were spirit too, but yet, I could not see through them. I could see my feet, legs, arms, and chest because I was not dressed in that three piece brown suit. I was bare foot, but I had some sort of clothing on that was not the suit I wore to church. I moved to the right and then to the left of the church and looked at all the people in attendance. I then moved back directly behind me and looked at my fleshly body in front of me. I knew then for sure that I was clearly out of my body. As I stood in the spirit body I could not see the people directly in front of my flesh body. Had I not left my flesh body I would be able to see the people in front of me. Then in one big rush of the spirit I was carried back into my flesh body. I stammered for a moment because all the while I was out of my body I could not remember a word I had spoken.

The out of body experience that Paul talked about is true. This further validates the scripture that an out of body experience is a reality. This, in line with many other experiences, has truly revolutionized my ministry. This out of body experience lasted about two to five minutes. It was one of the most magnificent supernatural experiences I ever had. But this was just the beginning of many supernatural dreams, visions and manifestations that would continue to take place. Glory be to Jehovah.

QUESTIONS FOR GROUP DISCUSSION:

1. Discuss Enoch's walk with God?
2. Elijah was carried away (2 Kings 2:11). Constrast this with Paul being caught up (2 Corinthians 12:2).
3. How would you describe the "rapture"?

CHAPTER

The Holy Ghost in the Hall

God is Spirit, and those who worship Him
must worship in spirit and truth.
John 4:24

My second visible manifestation of the Holy Ghost in 1982. I was the assistant pastor of Welcome Baptist Church in Fairmont, West Virginia. From the middle seventies I had been doing a lot fasting. I would fast many times for three to five days at a time and sometimes longer. Fasting had become a discipline that I enjoyed very much. Most of the fasts consisted of no food just water, but these only lasted three days. During these times of fasting, the Lord God would reveal many spiritual secrets to me. He would often visit me in dreams and reveal His will for my life. These were exciting times, and the Lord was active at Welcome Baptist Church with signs and wonders.

On June 11, 1982 the Holy Ghost spoke to me these words "your time has come." I really did not know what to make of such a pronouncement and what it really meant. But I was soon to find out what my future and this pronouncement would entail. God began to start moving in a mighty way at the church. Although I was the assistant pastor of a Baptist church, I attended a Pentecostal church in the evenings. During this part of my early ministry I had an intense desire for more of God. It was a hunger and thirst that never went away. Early in the morning or late at night it was a burning in my spirit for more of God. This passionate desire consisted of many days of fasting, praying, and reading the Bible until the early hours of the morning. As the prophet Isaiah stated, your mind should be focused on the Lord (Isaiah 26:3). My mind stayed on the Lord twenty-four hours a day, seven days a week. I could not get my mind off God. When I met with my friends, all I talked about was God. My thoughts, actions, demeanor longed to live the life of Christ.

During this time I was doing a lot of evangelistic work in nursing homes and hospitals. I would often preach in many denominational churches. Occasionally, I would preach out of town. The pastor of Welcome Baptist Church, the Reverend James Jackson and I saw the mighty hand of God move at this church. The hand of God moved with signs, wonders and healings whether in the Sunday morning service or the Wednesday night prayer meeting. Many Christians heard about what God was doing at the church. On Sunday mornings we would, for the most part, have a full church. A great deal of the congregation consisted of visitors from other churches. They came because of the miracles and healings that Jesus was performing. Even on Wednesday nights we had a full church of visitors.

Typically, after the morning preaching, we would ask if there was anyone who desired prayer. Many would come and we provided chairs in front of the congregation for them to sit down. We would anoint them with oil and I would walk the aisles until I felt the anointing. Once I felt the anointing of God, I would lay hands on them and pray. Many times I would not pray at all but just declare that they were healed and the Lord God would heal them.

It was during this period of time of great hunger and thirst for God that my focus turned to the Holy Ghost. I began to start reading books about the Holy Ghost and speaking in tongues. While attending Trinity Fellowship Church at night, I began to get acquainted with the Holy Ghost. The Reverend Jim Mease was the pastor who welcomed me with open arms. The people at the church were kind, loving and caring. I had never felt such love and caring from any other church. This hunger and thirst increased daily for the Holy Ghost. My thoughts stayed on Him. Every morning as well as during the day I would think about the Holy Ghost. I would often pray for the Holy Ghost to manifest Himself with signs and wonders. My wife and I would have long discussions regarding the Holy Ghost's ministry in the Church.

Reverend Mease, would discuss many topics regarding the Holy Ghost. Most of these topics were discussed on Sunday evenings at the evangelistic service. During this time I spent a lot time praying and seeking the face of God. Often I would be asked to preach the evangelistic service which I was more than happy to do. It was also during this time that my knowledge and some personal experiences with the Holy Ghost began to increase mightily. I was just ecstatic at the wealth of knowledge that seemed to flow into my spirit. The Holy Ghost was revealing God to me in word as well as deed. Many times I would go to church to pray, mostly in the evenings. While praying into the late hours of the evening, many supernatural manifestations would take place.

One evening I saw something that totally amazed me. As I walked toward the front of the church down the middle aisle, I saw a bright light glowing on the wall. In the front of the church there was a brown cross that stood about ten feet high. I walked toward the cross and as I came closer to it a bright light shone across the cross. The light was very bright. The light began to move in streaks across the back of the church exceedingly fast. Then as quickly and unexpectedly as it appeared the light disappeared. This one experience was the beginning of many such experiences that would take place at Trinity Fellowship Church.

It was July 22 and it started out like any other day with prayer early in the morning and Bible reading. Then off to work as usual then return home to continue my second session of prayer for the day. My wife, Nancy and I discussed the day's activities. As was the case nothing remarkable had taken place during the course of the day for either of us. After dinner I drove to Morris Park, a city municipal park, for my evening prayer session. I would often pray there because of the many secluded wooded areas. After having returned from the park, I prepared for bed and prayed again.

I was in the kitchen getting a glass of water and as I entered the hallway my eyes gazed upon a man. This in fact was not a man of flesh and blood but a man that was spirit. Even though this man was pure spirit, I could visibly see He was a man. I immediately felt this was the Holy Ghost. I could remember my first encounter with the Holy Ghost. Now, six years later, I was standing in the hallway of another home and the Holy Ghost was in the hall with me. I looked at Him and He looked at me. What a tremendous manifestation that was! The Holy Ghost was enveloped in light from His head to His toes. He did not have a color as white, black or brown but had a tint of gray. His presence was of power, authority, love, and kindness. This doesn't adequately describe this second manifestation of the Holy Ghost which was even more dramatic than the first. This was because I could see His entire person from head to toe without any obstructions. How would I describe the Holy Ghost? The Holy Ghost is God with the shape and image of a man in pure spirit. Jesus says, "God is a Spirit and they that worship him must worship Him in Spirit and in Truth" (John 4:24). Standing face to face with God is a hallowing experience that exceeds my greatest thoughts of God.

This experience with the Holy Ghost only kindled a fire that was a blaze for Jesus Christ already existing in my spirit. My thoughts of meeting God, the Holy Ghost, in the hall are many. My first thought was "why has God chosen me to manifest himself?" I am just a God-fearing minister who loves God with all my heart. I possess no special qualities, talents, or attributes that God would honor and bless me with this manifestion. Secondly, why did the Holy Ghost visit me and for what purpose? I really have no answer to this question. The Holy Ghost, for reasons only He knows, manifested himself to me. I can only guess why He has appeared to me in this fashion. I'm not sure if this manifestation was meant to bolster, increase, or cement my faith in God. I can only say that this manifestation of the Holy Ghost truly energized my Christian walk. I never doubted that God existed for one moment. Now, that I have seen him face-to-face, it has definitely reinforced my love for God. At that particular time I was unaware that within a matter of weeks I would experience another visible manifestation of the Holy Ghost of greater magnitude.

Questions for Group Discussion:

1. How important is prayer in your life?
2. How important is fasting in your life?
3. Have you ever felt the presence of the Holy Ghost? Describe this experience.

CHAPTER

The Dreams or Dreamer

Look, I have dreamed another dream
Exodus 37:9

Dreams—they all have meaning of something seen while asleep. The Holy Bible records 24 dreamers and 34 recorded dreams. There are 22 dreams recorded in the Old Testament and 12 dreams recorded in the New Testament. Dreams can reveal warnings, knowledge and even prophetic events from God. It is essential for ministers involved in the prophetic ministry to hear from God. All true prophets are called of God and are given His revelations and personal guidance. (Acts 3:21 and Hebrews 1:1-3). God often reveals Himself in dreams or visions as seen in Numbers 12:6.

The book of Job reveals to us that God speaks to men in dreams. "For God speaketh once, yea twice, yet man perceiveth it not" (Job 33:14). God often speaks to men in dreams, but men do not know or understand that God is talking to them because dream symbols require interpretation. They often pass it off as something that does not pertain to them or their family. God in dreams wants to reveal His will and purpose to man, but often man will reject God's will and purpose in his life and will not listen. "In a dream, in a vision of the night, when deep sleep falleth upon men in slumberings upon the bed:" (Job 33:15). People will often say what's in a dream? Some try to rationalize the dream or vision on the basis of their own conscious behavior. God deals with our conscious as well as with our unconscious behavior. Job said that God does two things when He speaks in a dream. "Then he openeth the ears of men and sealeth their instruction" (Job 33:16). First, God opens the ears of men in a dream or vision so that he can hear what God has said. So often people discount the supernatural because their lives are entrenched in the natural. The lives of everyday people are so experience oriented that only tangible things will satisfy them. Secondly, God said He will seal their instructions. God will give them instruction and seal it in their spirit never to be forgotten. God, in dreams and visions, is often giving instructions, warnings, comfort, and knowledge of past, present and future events.

In the New Testament we have God revealing His purpose and will for Joseph. Mary, the mother of Jesus, was espoused to Joseph. Before they came together, she was found with child of the Holy Ghost. Joseph being a just man and not willing to make Mary a public example was going to put her away privately. Then God appeared to Joseph in a dream to reveal His will and purpose to him. "But while he thought on these things, behold the Angel of the Lord appeared unto him in a dream saying, Joseph, thou son of David, fear not to take unto thee Mary thy wife; for that which is conceived in her is of the Holy Ghost" (Matthew 1:20).

This is the first of four times that the angel of the Lord appeared to Joseph in a dream. God's will and purpose for Joseph was not to put Mary away privately for conceived in her was Jesus by the Holy Ghost. God spoke to Joseph in a dream to reveal to him what His eternal purpose was. That purpose was that Jesus Christ, His Son, would be born to save his people from their sins. God gave Joseph special instructions that the baby should be named Jesus. Joseph being raised from sleep obeyed the Angel of God and took Mary to be his wife.

God reveals Himself again to Joseph—this time with a warning. God, in this dream, gives Joseph a personal warning and special instructions for their safety. Joseph, being the righteous man that he was, obeyed the word of God to the saving of his entire family. "And when they were departed, behold, the Angel of the Lord appeareth to Joseph in a dream, saying, arise, and take the young child and his mother and flee unto Egypt: and be thou there until I bring thee word: for Herod will seek the young child to destroy him" (Matthew 2:13). God gave explicit instructions to Joseph as to what He wanted him to do. Joseph believed the dreams as being from God and obeyed them to the very letter. God warned Joseph that Herod would seek the young Jesus to destroy him. God was saying if Herod found him he would kill Jesus and probably them also. Joseph, being a righteous and obedient man, obeyed God and rose quickly and he took the young child and his mother by night, and departed into Egypt (Matthew 2:14). Joseph did not hesitate when God spoke to him in dreams, but rather obeyed immediately. God often speaks in dreams, but how often do we listen and obey?

"But when Herod was dead, behold, an Angel of the Lord appeareth in a dream to Joseph in Egypt" (Matthew 2:19). God here again came to Joseph after a number of years had passed to give him further instructions. This appears to be the way that God spoke with and instructed Joseph in His will and purpose. God spoke to Joseph in definite terms with complete instructions and explanations. "Saying, arise, and take the young child and his mother, and go into the land of Israel: for they are dead which sought the young child's life" (Matthew 2:20). Joseph, having heard the instructions and commands of the Angel of the Lord, proceeded to the land of Israel. "And he arose and took the young child and his mother, and came into the land of Israel" (Matthew 2:21). Joseph's obedience to all God's commands proved that he was a man of good character and consecration. Having been warned in a dream, Joseph turned aside into the parts of Galilee and dwelt in a city called Nazareth.

Peter, in the Acts of the Apostles, quoted the prophet Joel. "And it shall come to pass in the last days, saith God, I will pour out of my Spirit upon all flesh: and your sons and daughters shall prophesy, and your young men shall see visions, and your old men shall dream dreams" (Acts 2:17).

On the day of Pentecost this was fulfilled and Peter quoted the Prophet Joel (Joel 2:28-29). Young men would see God given visions that was the purpose and will of God. Old men would dream dreams that was the purpose and will of God.   God over the years has spoken often to me in dreams.

Early Saturday morning September 18, 1982 God revealed His will and purpose for me in a series of dreams. A great number of people of all colors and races were chasing me. I permitted them to catch me without a struggle. They took me and placed me on a cross that was laying on the ground. Although I wasn't struggling to get up, a number of people held me down on the cross. I watched as a man proceeded to take from a bag nails that were very long and sharp. He took one of the nails along with a large hammer and proceeded to drive the nail into my right hand. I laid there on the cross as large amounts of blood gushed from my hand. The incredible thing was that there was no pain as I gazed upon the nail. Then the man with the hammer and nails moved to my left hand. The people who held my right hand also moved over to the left side and held my left hand down. Then the man with the bag of nails took one and pounded it into my left hand. The blood immediately gushed out of it and flowed profusely to the ground. As with the right hand the nail in the left hand did not cause any pain. Then the man and those holding my left hand moved to my feet. The man with the bag removed a nail and started hammering the nail into my feet. Like my right and left hands my feet bled profusely but there was no pain.

    This large group of people then set the cross up with me nailed to it. In the distance I could see a hill, and another erect cross with a man nailed to it. People were standing around his cross as they were standing around my cross. They were looking up at his cross as well as mine with their voices raised in anger. As I gazed upon the man nailed to the cross I could not see his face. His cross was not facing mine so I could not see who they had nailed there.

    God was revealing to me in this dream that as they had crucified Jesus, they will crucify me. It was being revealed to me that I would be crucified for my testimony of Jesus

Christ. God was warning me as a minister this would happen to me for preaching the truth. God had revealed his purpose and will to me in this particular dream.

This same morning God revealed other startling things to me in a dream: I saw three babies lined up in a row facing me. The babies on the end were the same size and they looked exactly alike. The baby in the middle had a much larger head than those on the end. Only the faces of the babies could be seen. The babies appeared to have faces of an adult, but one could recognize them as young. The babies were all smiling at me but none said a word as their grins grew larger. Their eyes glowed as bright as the sun as I stood there watching these babies without bodies. Their color was not black or white, but took on a variety of colors that appeared to my eyes as a pinkish-brown hue.

The smiling faces represent God's pleasure with me and the church. The eyes aglow represents the all seeing majesty and brightness of power and purity in the Godhead. The pinkish-brown color of God in many tints represents God is not a respecter of persons or colors.

This would not be the end of many dreams that God would reveal to me in the future. God does reveal His purpose and will to men in dreams.

Questions for Group Discussion:

1. Are all dreams from God?
2. How do you determine if a dream is from God, your subconscious, or from some other source?
3. Are there special people who can interpret dreams?

CHAPTER

The Vision

*After these things the word of the Lord
came to Abram in a vision
Genesis 15:1*

The Holy scriptures are replete with men who have experienced visions from God. In the Old Testament as well as in the New Testament men and women have experienced visions.

There are basically four types of visions that men and women have experienced. The first is the open vision where one is completely conscious and has his eyes open. The second is the vision where the person has his eyes closed but is still fully conscious. The third is when one is asleep and a vision appears before them. The fourth is when one is in a trance having lost all sense of consciousness.

Abram had just defeated a number of kings who had taken Lot, Abram's brother's son. Abram was no stranger to God because God often spoke with Abram. "After these things the word of the Lord came unto Abram in a vision saying, Fear not, Abram: I am thy shield, and thy exceeding great reward" (Genesis 15:1).

Let's look at exactly how the word of the Lord came to Abram. In a night vision the word of the Lord came to Abram to give him strength. Abram is one of 21 men who had visions from God in the Holy Bible. Abram was visited in a night vision to be encouraged by God. He told Abram in this vision to fear not. Generally, God says fear not when He wants to quiet someone because of His presence. People usually become excited and fearful in the presence of God and Abram was no exception. God appeared to Abram in this night vision to give him some great news. God says "I am thy shield, and thy exceeding great reward." God says as his shield He will protect and defend him if he puts all of his trust in Him. The shield protects the man's body and other essential parts from weapons and arrows from the enemy. God is a shield to all who trust and obey His commandments. God in this vision was Abram's exceeding great reward if he only trusted and obeyed Him.

Let's look at a vision that Jacob experienced. In Jacob's night vision God came to give him guidance and peace of mind. "And God spoke unto Israel in the visions of the night, and said, Jacob, Jacob. And he said, Here am I" (Genesis 46:2). God called Jacob by name twice in this night vision. God told Jacob He was the God of His father, the God of Isaac. After God introduced Himself, He told Jacob not to fear in going down to Egypt because He was with him. Isaac, Jacob's father, was forbidden by God to go down to Egypt (Genesis 26:2), but God told Jacob that it was His will for him to go down to Egypt. Jacob had doubts and fears about going to Egypt and the resettlement of his tribe there. The appearance of God was to assure him, and also give him a great promise. "And he said, I am God, the God of thy father, fear not to go down into Egypt; for I will there make of thee a great nation" (Genesis 46:3). God gives Jacob great assurance in that He will go with him, and that his son Joseph would close his eyes when he died. It was the custom that the nearest of kin would close the eyes and kiss the corpse of a loved one who died. Jacob would see his son whom he thought had been dead for many years. God told Jacob that he would go down with him into Egypt. God also told him that He would bring the nation of Israel out again.

Isaiah the prophet received an open vision from God. "The vision of Isaiah, the son of Amoz, which he saw concerning Judah and Jerusalem in the days of Uzziah, Jotham, Ahaz, and Hezekiah, Kings of Judah" (Isaiah 1:1). Isaiah received, whether by dream, revelation or mentally, certain prophecies from God. The scripture says he saw as by a vision or mental picture a revelation from God.

Nebuchadnezzar, King of Babylon, had a dream and was troubled and could not sleep. He summoned his wise men to interpret the dream. The wise men of his kingdom could not interpret the dream because they did not know what the king had dreamt. The king declared that if an interpretation could not be given that they would all perish. Daniel went to the king and desired that the king would give him more time and he would show him the interpretation. Daniel went to his three companions, Hananiah, Mishael, and Azariah and made known to them the situation. God moved on behalf of Daniel and his three companions." Then was the secret revealed unto Daniel in a night vision. Then Daniel blessed the God of heaven" (Daniel 2:19).

What did Daniel and his three companions do that others probably would not have done? Daniel desired the mercies of the God of heaven. How was this done? Daniel, Hananiah, Mishael, and Azariah prayed that same night that God would give them the dream. Then God revealed the secret to Daniel in a night vision, and Daniel blessed the God of heaven. Daniel then revealed the dream to King Nebuchadnezzar "But there is a God in heaven that revealeth secrets, and maketh known to the King Nebuchadnezzar what shall be in the latter days. Thy dream, and thy bed, are these..." (Daniel 2:28). Before Daniel gave the king the answer he first gave God the glory. He told the king God is the only true God and that God, the God of heaven, was greater than all the wise men on the earth. Primarily the entire object of the dream was to reveal to Nebuchadnezzar what would befall his kingdom after his death. Also it was to reveal all the world empires from then to the dateless future. Daniel said it was a vision for the later days of the king's kingdom after his death.

On a Wednesday night, September 22, 1982, we held our prayer and Bible study service and the Lord God revealed this tremendous open vision to me. As a youngster I attended some movies and I always sat in the front seats to see the big picture. This night in church it was as if I was on this big movie screen as this vision unfolded. I was at a city owned municipal park in Fairmont called Morris Park. I saw myself down on my knees as if I was praying to God. Then out of nowhere a large group of angels with large wings approached me as I continued to pray. One angel had a large cross in his right hand and he approached me to touch me. He placed on my forehead the large cross that he had in his right hand. The angel held the cross upon my forehead as it burned a mark into my head. After about twenty seconds the angel lifted the cross from my forehead as I continued to pray with my hands raised. Smoke seemed to rise from my forehead as the mark from the cross was branded into my head. While I was watching this vision take place on this big screen I was in the Spirit. The angels ascended into heaven and the one with the cross in his hand was the last to ascend. They ascended until they were completely out of sight and then the vision ended. This revealed to me that God had sealed me unto the day of redemption. This cross of Christ branded into my forehead as a mark implies that I belonged to Him forever. The prayer service ended and I never said a word to any one about this vision. This was just one of many such visions that would take place in my ministry.

QUESTIONS FOR GROUP DISCUSSION:

1. Are all visions from God?
2. What is the difference between a dream and a vision?
3. God not only gave Daniel the interpretation of Nebuchadnezzar's dream, but what the king had dreamt. Why do you think the king would not tell the wise men the dream?

CHAPTER

God Heals My Mother

*So He touched her hand, and the fever left her.
And she arose and served them.
Matthew 8:15*

Jesus was anointed with the Holy Ghost to minister to mankind. "How God anointed Jesus of Nazareth with the Holy Ghost and with power; who went about doing good, and healing all that were oppressed of the devil: for God was with him" (Acts 10:38). Jesus left His glory with God the Father in heaven. "And now, O Father, glorify thou me with thine own self with the glory which I had with thee before the world was" (John 17:5). Jesus was with the Father in Glory in the pre-existence of the world. Jesus came to earth in the likeness of sinful flesh. "For what the law could not do in that it was weak through the flesh, God sending his own Son in the likeness of sinful flesh, and for sin, condemned sin in the flesh" (Romans 8:3). The law was weak in the flesh. It just could not permanently forgive sins. The law absolutely had no power to control the flesh, because sin already controlled it before the law was established. Sin within itself would not allow the flesh to be obedient to the law. God had to make a plan for man's salvation from sin so that the flesh could be set free to fulfill the righteousness the law required.

Jesus was not sin and had not sinned but had to die for

sinful mankind. "And being found in fashion as a man, he humbled himself, and became obedient unto death, even the death of the cross" (Philippians 2:8). Jesus, who, being in the form of God, took the form of a bondservant, and coming in the likeness of men, humbled himself from the divine deity to become man. He humbled himself to the point of being crucified on the cross bearing the sins of all mankind. Jesus was tempted in all points as we are tempted. "For we have not a high priest which cannot be touched with the feeling of our infirmities; but was in all points tempted like as we are, yet without sin" (Hebrews 4:15). Jesus Christ is our high priest, and He was tempted in all things like mankind but He did not consent to sin. Jesus is our pattern and perfect example. "For even hereunto were ye called: because Christ also suffered for us, leaving us an example, that ye should follow his steps" (1 Peter 2:21). As Christians we will suffer and endure many hardships, thus following Christ. Christ is our example and we should, as Christians, continue to walk in his footsteps.

Jesus was anointed by God (Acts 10:38) to minister and perform miracles. Jesus, with this anointing, performed His first miracle after He was thirty years of age. "This beginning of miracles did Jesus in Cana of Galilee, and manifested for his glory; and his disciples believed on him" (John 2:11). What was this miracle that Jesus performed under the anointing of the Holy Ghost? Jesus' first miracle was turning six water pots of water into 162 gallons of wine.

Later in Jesus' ministry, Peter's mother-in-law was in danger of death because of a great fever. "And he arose out of the synagogue, and entered into Simon's house.

And Simon's wife's mother was taken with a great fever; and they besought him for her" (Luke 4:38). Jesus had just delivered a man from an unclean devil (Luke 4:33-37). Jesus entered into Simon's house were he found Simon's mother-in-law. Someone had called for Jesus and He promptly went to Simon Peter's house. "And he stood over her, and rebuked the fever; and it left her: and immediately she arose and ministered unto them" (Luke 4:39). Jesus was fearless of any infectious diseases and He demonstrated complete power over them. Jesus rebuked the fever and it left her immediately. She may have washed their feet, or she may have prepared them a large meal. She was completely healed by Jesus and her ministering to them proved it.

God has healed many people in my ministry including my mother. This happened on a Tuesday, September 29, 1982. My mother, Rose Lee Moody, called early in the morning. Her voice was a voice of someone in extreme pain. While talking to her on the telephone, her voice was unusually soft and trembling. I knew that something was seriously wrong with her because she was always spirited. She started out by complaining about having severe pains in her lower stomach. My mother instructed me to go to my sister, Corliss Bridges' home. Charlotte Moody, another one of my sisters, had left for class at Fairmont State College. My mother wanted Rosemary and Charlotte to take her to the hospital to be admitted. I left my home in Fairmont and drove as fast as I could to my mother's house in Grant Town. I helped her put on some clothes and pack a suitcase for her hospital stay. I noticed that she was constantly complaining about how severe the pain had become in her stomach. I secured my mother's house and we started for Fairmont General Hospital as quickly as we could. While driving to the hospital, the Spirit of God said "anoint her head with oil." So I stopped the car anointed her head with oil and began to pray for her beside the road. We arrived in Fairmont and went to my sister, Corliss' house. I left her in the car for a moment while I went up to inform Corliss and Rosemary of her condition. Corliss immediately dressed, and we left her house and drove mother straight to the hospital.

While at the hospital the Spirit of the Lord spoke to me and told me to "pray for her again." I prayed for my mother again as the Spirit of the Lord had instructed me. They had put my mother on a stretcher, and I was instructed to read Psalm 91 which I did. They admitted her. Corliss and I stayed for an hour. I left the hospital drove home and changed clothes. Nancy and Kris, my son, went back to the hospital with me. We arrived at 11:00 a.m. and we went immediately to her room.

My mother told me that the pain was gone and the knot that was visibly about the size of a soft ball was gone. My mother had a very large hernia, which is nothing more than the protrusion of the intestine through the wall surrounding it. The doctors operated on my mother that same day only to find out that she was completely healed. The hernia had completely disappeared, and they found no evidence that she ever had a hernia. When the doctors revealed this to us, we gave God the praise and the glory for the healing. They kept my mother for a few days for observation and then released her. She was completely healed.

My mother has never ever complained about that pain again. Praise be to God. This would be only the beginning of many miracles and healings.

Questions for Group Discussion:

1. What is your first reaction when facing sickness or pain?
2. Is suffering from God?
3. What does Jesus say about healing?
4. Does God heal everyone who asks? Did Jesus heal everyone in His earthly ministry?

CHAPTER 11

Attacked By Devils

For with authority and power He commands
the unclean spirits, and they come out.
Luke 4:36

The Holy Bible is replete with cases of people who have been oppressed and possessed with devils. Israel committed many sins against God. One of those sins was sacrificing to devils. "Yea, they sacrificed their sons and their daughters unto devils" (Psalm 106:37). The word devils appear four times in the Old Testament and 51 times in the New Testament. The devils referred to in the Old testament are in fact familiar spirits. These devils are the supernatural spirits that are involved in witchcraft.

God commanded Moses to speak to Aaron about making sacrifices to Him in the Tabernacle (Leviticus 17:1-6). God wanted the people to make sacrifices to Him in the tabernacle and not in an open field. Many people of the house of Israel had been offering up sacrifices to devils in the open fields. God wanted to totally put an end to any sacrifices to devils anywhere. "And they shall no more offer their sacrifices unto devils, after whom they have gone a whoring. This shall be a statute forever unto them throughout their generations" (Leviticus 17:7). The house of Israel offered pagan sacrifices and worshipped devils and not Jehovah. In Hebrew the word devils is *sa'ir* which is shaggy he-goat, satyr, rough and hairy. The house of Israel was very stiffnecked and rebellious toward Jehovah. We can see a total lack of appreciation for God demonstrated by Israel. "They provoked him to jealousy with strange gods, with abominations provoked they him to anger" (Deuteronomy 32:16). The house of Israel (Jeshurum) is a symbolic name of Israel meaning the upright one. They forsook God, rejected the Rock of their salvation and provoked Him with their sinning. They provoked God to jealousy with serving many strange gods. God had given them the best crops, the best places on earth and a huge increase in their fields (Deuteronomy 32:13). They provoked God to anger with many abominations. They committed such abominations as making images, idols of Ammon, idols of Moab, idols of Zidon, eating unclean things, offering human sacrifices, robbery and murder. This is just a short list of 31 abominations that provoked Him to anger.

"They sacrificed unto devils, not to God: to gods whom they knew not, to new gods that came newly up, whom your fathers feared not" (Deuteronomy 32:17). They sacrificed to devils; and every new god that rose up they sacrificed to it. The house of Israel like many in the church today have forgotten God and serve the gods of materialism. "Of the Rock that begot thee thou art unmindful, and hast forgotten God that formed thee" (Deuteronomy 32:18). The house of Israel was truly blessed because they had been born of God anew. God had begotten them and formed them, yet, they were forgetful and unattentive of Him.

❖

In the Old Testament the house of Israel sacrificed unto devils. In the New Testament these devils are called unclean spirits and familiar spirits. Jesus, when He walked upon the earth, was anointed by God to cast out devils as seen in Acts 10:38. In the gospel according to Saint Matthew it makes reference to Jesus' ability to cast out devils. "When the even was come, they brought unto him many that were possessed with devils: and he cast out the spirits with his word and healed all that were sick" (Matthew 8:16). Many that were possessed with devils were brought to Jesus. During that period in Israel many of the people were oppressed and possessed with devils. Matthew says that Jesus cast out the spirits with his word. Jesus anointed with the Holy Ghost has power over all devils and supernatural evil. The gospel according to Saint Luke refers to Jesus casting out an unclean devil in the synagogue. "And in the synagogue there was a man, which had a spirit of an unclean devil, and cried out with a loud voice" (Luke 4:33).

This proves that many today have unclean spirits that attend church on a regular basis. Thousands of Christians around the world are possessed by unclean devils of which many are unaware. This unclean devil was impure, lewd, and foul with the ability to speak out loud. This unclean devil had possessed this man taking complete control of his body and vocal cords. "Saying, Let us alone; what have we to do with thee, thou Jesus of Nazareth? art thou come to destroy us? I know thee who thou art; the Holy One of God" (Luke 4:34). The unclean devil speaks asking Jesus the question, "What have we to do with thee, thou Jesus of Nazareth?" This unclean spirit speaks, and he is not alone for he says, "Let us alone" (verse 34). They knew that Jesus was going to deal with them in some manner.

Jesus will deal with all unclean spirits one day as they will be locked away for good. They were concerned that Jesus was going to destroy them because they knew who he was. They knew that Jesus was the Holy One of God, the Son of God. This unclean devil was able to recognize who Jesus was, but many in Israel were blind to who Jesus was. Many people today still do not recognize that Jesus is the Holy One of God. Jesus would not let the unclean spirit speak any further. "And Jesus rebuked him, saying, hold thy peace, and come out of him. And when the devil had thrown him in the midst, he came out of him, and hurt him not" (Luke 4:35). In effect he told them to be muzzled and speak no more. These unclean devils are intelligent beings capable of speaking. These unclean devils were obedient to Jesus. These unclean devils enter men (possess them), depart from them, and can cause many physical problems. It appears that the man suffered some sort of convulsion when the devil threw him into the midst. As Jesus commanded the unclean devil departed from the man without any harm coming to the man.

This experience with unclean devils took place October 22, 1982 in McKeesport, Pennsylvania. Pastor, Dorothy Reeves, my sister, invited me to preach and minister at a monthly prayer breakfast.

As I was laying on the bed meditating about tomorrow's prayer breakfast, for about two minutes, out of the clear night in my room three unclean devils appeared like snakes. They were brown and green in color with brown spots on each of them. They were about five to six feet long and resembled many snakes I have seen. These unclean devils were moving very fast and coming toward me. They began to speak with a loud audible voice, each one speaking something different. I commanded the three unclean devils to, "Get behind me Satan." This did not stop them. As they came closer, they entered my throat and paralyzed me. I felt a very sharp pain when the three unclean devils entered my throat. The pain was very sharp and extended into my neck and spinal column. This pain in my neck and spine felt like an enormous explosion. A large cramp developed in my throat, and I was unable to speak or utter a sound. This appeared to have lasted at least two or more minutes as I lay there in pain on the bed. Again I prayed to God, and the pain and the devils departed from my throat. That was one of the most unbelievable experiences I ever had. That night I lay awake watching the room to see if these unclean devils would return. I neither heard nor saw any more unclean devils that night. The most fascinating thing about the experience was the ability of these three unclean devils to speak so plainly.

About an hour later I fell asleep and had a very enjoyable sleep. I woke up about 6:00 a.m. showered and got dressed. Before leaving the house I drank a glass of orange juice and a cup of coffee. We then departed from McKeesport and drove to Pittsburgh. We arrived in Pittsburgh about 7:20 a.m. The church where the prayer breakfast was held is New Light Temple Baptist Church. One of the first to arrive that morning was the Reverend Charles K. White from Houston. Reverend White had moved from Texas and resided in Pittsburgh. We had a very extensive and meaningful conversation for about fifteen minutes before pastor Reverend George Gamble arrived. Pastor Gamble opened the breakfast with prayer and we had a refreshing time.

After breakfast the pastor and I went upstairs to start the morning worship service. Dorothy opened the morning worship service with songs and testimonies. Pastor Gamble stood and began speaking in tongues and prophesying. While he was speaking in tongues and prophesying he started jumping up and down. This amazed me to see someone jumping up and down while speaking in tongues because I had never seen this before. Dorothy then introduced me as the speaker for the morning worship service. I preached from James 1:22 as God greatly anointed me to expound on His word with great power. I gave an altar call but no one came. So I had the deacons line up twelve chairs up front. I told the congregation if anyone needed prayer, to come and sit in one of the chairs. Slowly one by one they came up and sat in the chairs in front of the altar. I anointed each person with oil on their foreheads in the name of the Lord. I got down on my knees to pray, putting my right hand on their head. I then held their hand with my left hand and started praying.

As I started praying, the first person "fell" under the power of God in her chair. Then like dominoes the others in the chairs began "to fall" under the power of God. Some fell on the floor, and some slumped in their chairs. Reverend Gamble, who had been ministering with me started speaking in tongues and prophesying again. We went down the line helping those up who had fallen under the power of God. Many people desired prayer that day and as we prayed, God healed them. Many in the two and half hour service were healed and fell under the power of God.

As I looked back at the night before, I knew why I was attacked by those three unclean devils. They did not want me to speak God's word and pray for the many people that came for healing. This was not my last encounter with unclean devils, as I would encounter many more.

QUESTIONS FOR GROUP DISCUSSION:

1. How would you define materialism?
2. How do the cares of life affect your walk with God?
3. Ephesians 6:12 describes our battle with the enemy. What remedies do you find in Ephesians 6:13-18, Luke 10:19, and Psalm 91?

CHAPTER

Voices, Voices, Voices

The eyes of the Lord are in every place,
Keeping watch on the evil and the good.
Proverbs 15:3

Voice or speech can be defined as the ability to produce a sound expressed in a vocal utterance. Man, animals, supernatural beings and God have the ability to speak with an audible voice.

In Genesis chapter three we have an amazing account of God the Father, the serpent, the woman, and Adam speaking. In this chapter we have man's failure that is his temptation and his fall. The chapter starts out with the serpent, described as a very subtle beast of the field. The serpent began conversing with the woman about trees in the Garden of Eden. The woman replied to the serpent the command of God (Genesis 2:15-17). The serpent told the woman if she ate of the tree she would not die, but their eyes would be opened and they would be gods and God knew it.

The serpent's temptation demonstrates his shrewdness. His motive was merely to cause the fall of mankind. When the serpent told the woman she would not die, this was the first lie in scripture. The enemy, satan often appeals to man to make a god out of himself. The serpent appealed to the woman's fleshy desire to be a god. Scripture says the woman saw that the tree was good for food. It was pleasant to the eyes and a tree to make one wise. She took the fruit, ate it, and gave it to her husband who was with her, and he also ate.

Adam and Eve faced a three-fold temptation. First, they were tempted by the lust of the flesh when she saw the tree was good for food. Second, they were tempted by the lust of eyes when she saw it was pleasant to look on. Third, they were tempted by the pride of life when she saw it would make one wise. There is one startling question that one might ask — what was Adam saying and doing during the temptation? Adam was in the garden with Eve. So he was without excuse for the fall. Adam should have spoken up and defended and protected Eve from this temptation. Adam remained silent, for what reason? Was Adam afraid of the serpent or was Adam afraid to stop the woman? Nevertheless, Adam's failure to prevent this from happening left him equally as guilty. He could have refused the fruit whenever Eve offered it to him. But, he did not refuse the fruit that Eve offered him thus, ignoring God's command about it.

Scripture says the eyes of Adam and Eve were opened and they knew that they were naked. Before they sinned against God, their eyes were as pure as their hearts. After they sinned against God, their eyes were opened unto sin and corruption. Before they sinned against God, they were God aware. After they sinned against God, they lost their God awareness. They lost the ability to do the right things before God. They gained the ability to do and perfect the wrong things. Adam lost his wonderful sinlessness and gained an evil nature. Adam had the power like God only to do good, but he lost it when he sinned. They sewed fig leaves together, and made themselves aprons to hide and cover themselves. Sin was now out in the open and they became acutely aware of it. They heard the voice of the Lord God walking in the garden in the cool of the day.

God today often walks among us in some manifestation of which we are totally unaware. Adam knew the voice of God and actually saw God himself. When God formed every beast of the field and fowl of the air, according to scripture He brought them to Adam so he could name them. After their fall, Adam and Eve tried to hide from God among the trees in the garden after hearing the voice of God. They tried to hide from an all knowing and all seeing God which they found out they could not do.

In Proverbs 15:3 Solomon says the eyes of God are everywhere seeing the good and the bad. There was no place for them to hide although they truly tried. The Lord God called Adam and asked him where he was. God evidently addressed Adam by name and his response was, "I heard thy voice in the garden, and I was afraid."

Was it a voice of anger or guilt that caused Adam to be afraid? Adam then proceeded to confess to God the evil of his actions. First, he said I heard thy voice which is a recognition of God. Second, he said he was afraid. What was he afraid of? Third, he said he was naked. This is what happens when we sin against God. Fourth he said he hid himself. He hid because he was guilty of the sin he committed. Then God proceeded to ask Adam a series of questions concerning this sin.

God's second question was, "who told you that you were naked?" Before Adam had a chance to answer the question God answered the question with another question. God knew exactly what Adam had done even though

He asked the question. God expressly commanded Adam to never eat of that tree or he would surely die. Adam must have never thought or even reasoned within himself what death meant. Did God explain to Adam in great detail all the implications of death? God asked Adam "Has thou eaten of the tree, the one I commanded thee that thou should not eat?" Adam's response should have been yes to God instead of the one he gave. Adam's response to God was, "That woman you gave me, she gave it to me." Instead of taking full responsibility for the sin, Adam tried to put the blame on the woman. He had the audacity to slightly imply that maybe God was somewhat responsible. Maybe his thinking was that if God had not given him the woman he would not have succumbed to the temptation. Adam, like many others today, was trying to blame others for his guilt.

During this entire conversation with the serpent, Adam was present. Why was Adam silent during the temptation of his wife? Why did Adam let the woman walk to the tree, take fruit from it and then eat it? But a much greater question must be asked. Why did he accept the fruit from her and then eat it? Did his wife put some extreme pressure on him to eat the fruit? On the other hand, did he take it voluntarily, completely forgetting God's command about the tree?

So, Adam confessed that the woman gave it to him and he in fact did eat it willingly. Then God again spoke to the woman. God said to the woman, "What is this thing that thou hast done?" The woman's response was that the serpent had beguiled her, and she did eat the fruit from the tree. As God continued He cursed the serpent next.

God said to the serpent, because you have done this

you are cursed above every beast of the field. God further told the serpent that upon his belly he would go and dust he would eat all the days of his life. This clearly tells us that the serpent walked upright before this great fall. God continued to speak and put a curse upon the serpent, the woman, the man, and the entire earth.

My personal experiences with audible voices is not just limited to a few isolated incidents. I have had many experiences where I heard many audible voices that spoke with me. The following experience is just one of these that took place in my life. It was October 29, 1982, in our home I was watching television downstairs in the family room with my youngest daughter, Kirsten. We watched television for about two hours when Kirsten fell asleep on the couch. I was sitting in a chair near the couch. I continued to watch television for about an hour, then decided to take Kirsten upstairs to bed after the television program was over. The other children were in bed asleep. I know this because I left the family room twice to check on them. I went to the couch, picked Kirsten up and proceeded upstairs to put her in bed.

As I reached the foyer I heard voices of about three to four angels talking in the hallway. As I stood there with Kirsten in my arms, I listened intently as these three or four angels spoke in audible voices. After listening for about three to five minutes, I moved toward the top of the stairs. The voices continued until I reached the top of the steps and then they suddenly stopped. I proceeded down the hall where I put Kirsten in her bed. I then closed the door to her room and immediately went to the other children's room. They were asleep, and I proved this by waking them up. They proceeded to ask me why I had awaken them out of their sleep. I closed the door to the room and listened for about two minutes to see if they were talking but they were not. I was fully convinced that three to four angels were talking that night in the hallway. It was a supernatural experience that I will never forget.

Questions for Group Discussion:

1. Have you ever heard voices when no one else was there?
2. Does God speak to everyone?
3. How does one discern the voice of God from the voice of the enemy?

CHAPTER

Jesus' Tomb

> Now in the place where He was crucified there was a garden, and in the garden a new tomb in which no one had yet been laid.
> John 19:41

Jesus died on the cross, and there was a rich man of Arimathaea named Joseph who desired Jesus' body (Matthew 27:57-66). The town of Arimathaea was some five miles north of Jerusalem. Joseph went to Pilate and asked for the body of Jesus, and Pilate commanded the body be delivered to him. Joseph then took the body and wrapped it in a clean linen cloth. He then laid Jesus' body in his own new tomb, which he had hewn out of the rock. Then a great stone was rolled against the door of the tomb.

Mary Magdalene and the other Mary were sitting opposit the tomb. The next day, which followed the day of preparation, the chief priests and pharisees came to Pilate and uttered these words, "We remember that this deceiver said while he was alive, after three days he would rise again." Even the Jews knew and understood the particulars of the three days and nights in the tomb. They knew full well that Jesus must be dead at least three full days and not one day and one night after his burial as some claim. The Jews wanted Pilate to make the tomb secure until the third day. They reasoned that Jesus' disciples would come at night and steal the body. Then Jesus' disciples would tell the people that Jesus had risen, so that the last error should be far worse than the first. So the Jews went and made the tomb secure by sealing the stone and setting up a watch. The stone had a government seal attached to each end to let them know if it had been removed.

In Saint Matthew chapter 28, verses one through seventeen, it gives us an angelic explanation of Jesus' resurrection. At the end of the Sabbath at dawn on the first day of the week which was Sunday, Mary Magdalene and the other Mary came to see the tomb. There was a great earthquake and an angel of the Lord descended from heaven and rolled back the stone from the door. Then the angel sat upon the stone. This was the second earthquake to take place in a matter of three days. The angel's face was like lightening and his clothes were as white as snow. This angel demonstrated great power as was represented on his face. His white garment demonstrated the purity and sinlessness of heaven. Great fear fell upon the guards and they shook and became as dead men. Seeing such a heavenly being put fear in their hearts causing them to shake and fall prostrate. The angel spoke to the women and told them not to fear, for he knew they sought Jesus who was crucified. The angel said that Jesus was not there for he had risen as he said. He invited them to see the place where the Lord had lain. The angel then told the women to go quickly and tell his disciples that Jesus has risen from the dead. He then gave them further instruction that Jesus was going ahead into Galilee, and when they arrived in Galilee they would see him. The angel closed with, "I have told you." The women were told to give the good news of Jesus' resurrection to his disciples. The angel of the Lord knew that the disciples were fearful and in doubt to the point of some severe skepticism. The angel wanted them to get the good news of the resurrection to stop the doubt, fearfulness and skepticism. The women quickly departed from the tomb with holy fear and great joy. They were running to bring the disciples the good news as told to them by the angel.

As the women went to tell his disciples, Jesus met them saying, "all hail" to get their attention. The women stopped at his command and held on to his feet and worshipped him greatly. Jesus told the women not to be afraid, but go tell his brethren to go to Galilee where they would see him. Even though the disciples in the past showed some cowardice with a large degree of unbelief, Jesus still loved them and had forgiven them. He met His eleven disciples in Galilee in a mountain that He had appointed. When the disciples saw Jesus they worshipped Him, but some of the disciples still doubted.

My supernatural experience with Jesus' tomb took place Sunday evening, January 16, 1983 at Trinity Fellowship Church. I rose early that Sunday morning for prayer and my daily Bible reading. I proceeded to wake my wife, Nancy and my three children for church. When we were all dressed we left the house and drove to Welcome Baptist Church for the morning service. The Holy Ghost blessed us in a mighty way that Sunday morning. With the gifts of the Spirit in operation I brought the morning sermon entitled "Yield Not to Temptation" as the Holy Ghost anointed me. The presence of the Holy Ghost in the service was a glorious manifestation of His blessedness.

The Reverend James Jackson and I laid hands on the sick and prayed for many with the Holy Ghost doing the work. I dismissed the morning service. We shook hands and hugged each other, then we departed. As I ate Sunday dinner with the family, I had no idea what God had in store for me. After dinner I took Kris and Kirsten to my sister, Corliss' house for the evening. Then I left for brother Jack Ward's house. Upon arriving at brother Ward's house I asked brother Ward would he be interested in visiting Trinity Fellowship Church that night. As I asked him this question the Spirit of God spoke to him and the power of God took him backwards into his bedroom. Brother Ward told me that he would go with me to Trinity Fellowship Church for the evening service. We arrived at the church around 6:00 p.m. and were greeted by Louise Green Brown and Reverend James Mease. The service started out just as many had in the past. We all stood and sang about five songs as the presence of the Lord became very intensified. After we had sung, Reverend Mease invited the congregation to come around the altar for prayer. I began with the others to raise my hands to God in prayer and praise. I must have prayed for about twelve minutes then we sang another few songs. I started to pray again with uplifted hands while praising God with all my might. Reverend Mease was speaking about the power and presence of the Holy Ghost.

Then one of the most spectacular series of supernatural events started to unfold. In the Spirit I was transported in front of this large motion picture screen. I could not see the inside of the church or the congregation or Reverend Mease speaking. The only thing I could see was this large motion picture screen completely white and shining. This reminded me of when I was a youngster going to the movies at the old Fairmont Theater in Fairmont. I would sit in the front so that the actors on screen would appear larger than life. Then as from nowhere I saw Jesus upon this large motion picture screen in a long white robe. Jesus radiated as the brilliance of the sun and His robe glistened in pure holiness. Jesus was walking down this road that was very straight and narrow. As Jesus walked down this road, He had a long staff in His hand that was whiter than white. Following behind Jesus was untold millions of sheep that seemed to stretch for miles. These sheep radiated with a similar brilliance that radiated from Jesus. I sat there in great amazement and watched this great supernatural vision unfold with divine reverence.

Then Jesus and the millions of sheep disappeared from the screen in the blinking of an eye. I then saw this very large white pitcher that glowed and gave off a very bright brilliance. This pitcher was held by a man's hand that was white as snow and it also glistened. This hand was the only thing I could see. It was as if this hand was detached from the man's entire body. The hand then raised the white pitcher from its resting position and tilted it forward. Simultaneously, I was projected upon this large motion picture screen with a pitcher or cup in my hand. As I stood there looking at this hand holding this white pitcher, he started to pour. The hand filled the pitcher I was holding until it overflowed to the ground. It overflowed until it ran and formed a very large stream that resembled a river. This large white pitcher contained either water or wine. I could not tell which. As I stood there, the hand continued to pour out the water or wine into my pitcher indefinitely. It covered my shoes and ran in large torrents to form a river. Then, as suddenly as it appeared, the hand and pitcher disappeared from the screen.

Then I saw some words appear on the big screen in front of me in big bold blackletters. The words were "Miracles and Healing." These two words remained on the screen for about twenty seconds then they vanished. What took place next was one of the most glorious supernatural experiences I have ever experienced.

As I sat there in my seat in front of this large screen, the tomb of Jesus suddenly appeared. I was transported from my seat onto the large screen and I was standing about twenty feet in front of Jesus' tomb. I saw an angel standing on the outside of the tomb near the door. He was clothed in a robe that shone like the brightness of the sun. From where I was standing I could see down inside the tomb of Jesus. Jesus was lying there apparently still dead. I then noticed another angel sitting at Jesus' head. This angel said nothing, but his eyes were intently focused on Jesus' body. Where the angels were sitting, I saw what appeared to be hay or straw. Then I saw Mary Magdalene and another woman down inside the tomb of Jesus standing at His feet. Christ was clothed in a very bright and radiant robe which was even brighter than the two angels rose as to be resurrected, sat up on His couch and stood to his feet. His eyes were fixed on me and my eyes were fixed on His as He started to walk up the stairs of the tomb. Jesus reached the top of the stairs, paused for a minute then started walking toward me. Jesus continued to walk toward me. When He was about three feet away from me He stopped abruptly. Jesus' eyes were fixed on mine and I continued to look upon him with holy reverence. Jesus stood directly in front of me for about one minute without saying a word. Then one of the most astounding supernatural things took place. Jesus started walking toward me again as I stood there, and then He walked into my body. Jesus Christ walked into my body in this vision. I felt His virtue, power, and divinity enter me. This was one of the greatest supernatural experiences I have ever had. After Jesus had entered into my body in the spirit I was transported back to Trinity Fellowship Church. I have no knowledge of how long my spirit had been out of my body. This was one of the most phenomenal supernatural experiences that God had revealed to me.

Questions for Group Discussion:

1. In John 15:4 Jesus says, "Abide in Me, and I in you." Discuss what it means to abide.
2. How often do you feel the presence of God in your own life?
3. How can you develop greater intimacy with Jesus?

CHAPTER 14

Manifestations of the Holy Ghost

For the kingdom of God is not in word but in power.
1 Corinthians 4:20

The Holy Ghost is also known as the Comforter who helps us in our daily Christian walk. The Holy Ghost has often manifested Himself to me whether at home or in a church service. In this chapter I will detail some further manifestations of the Holy Ghost in my ministry. It was Friday, April 29, 1983. I started my day at 6:00 a.m. with prayer and Bible reading. I read two lessons from Kenneth Hagin's book, "New Thresholds of Faith." This book has been very helpful to me over the years. It has greatly enhanced my spiritual growth in the area of faith.

In prayer I asked for more signs and wonders to follow my ministry. I also prayed that God's thoughts, ways and attitude would be my thoughts, ways and attitude. After prayer I decided I would go to Christian Unity Church for an B.Y.E. Gospel Train Service. Nancy and Alethea are members of the B.Y.E. Choir. Everywhere I go I keep a pen and note pad because God is always giving me revelations from His Spirit. We left the house and upon arriving at the church, Nancy and Alethea put on their choir robes in anticipation of the service. I took a seat and began to pray quietly in tongues. After about ten minutes the choir marched on to the choir stand. Nancy was the choir director. After about the sixth or seventh song the Spirit of God began giving me some revelations. I immediately started writing down all these revelations that He was giving me. There were a total of six revelations that the Spirit revealed to me. I will share these revelations with you.

First, the Holy Spirit revealed that Christian Unity Church had no power. In an audible voice I heard the words: they are backslidden and I have removed my presence from them. God was revealing to me that this church of water baptized believers had no supernatural power. This was a church full of emotion but not of the Holy Ghost and power. The choir sang, but the anointing was not on them; the ministers preached with no quickening power of the Spirit. They had some form of godliness, but the power was nonexistent. Paul says, "For the kingdom of God is not in word, but in power" (1 Corinthians 4:20). The Bible reveals five different kinds of power that the church has at its disposal. In other words, it was spiritually dead.

Second, the Holy Ghost revealed that this church needed to yield to the Spirit of God. In this revelation He spoke to me and said, they have forgotten me and are serving themselves for selfish ends. Paul speaks in Romans 6:12-14 about yielding and to whom to yield ourselves. Paul says in verse twelve that we should not let sin reign in our mortal bodies. He describes sin as the king that has the body, soul, and spirit of man under its control. Paul continues to stress not to give place to sin working in your life. Sin is a spirit that can rule and reign in our mortal bodies if permitted. In verse thirteen he exhorts them to not yield their bodies as instruments of unrighteousness unto sin. You do not sin when you are tempted, it is sin when you yield to the temptation. He tells them to yield themselves to God. We should yield our will to the will of God if we expect to refrain from sin. We are dead to sin and our bodies are to be used as instruments of righteousness unto God. Paul's reference to instruments is a reference to weapons that we should use to fight the devil. In verse fourteen he says sin shall not have dominion over you. If you are truly born again, God delivers you from sin in the body, soul and spirit. If you fall back into sin, it is your choice to do so. Paul concludes by saying you are not under the law, but under the grace of God.

Third, the Spirit spoke two words to me, "prophecy" and "prophet." In the word "prophesy" He told me that I would receive information from God about a person's life and that He would reveal things to me about the natural and spiritual world. In the word "prophet" I was told that I would be placed in the office of the prophet as an agent of God and commissioned to speak as He commands me to. Through the years God has used me many times in the office of a prophet.

Fourth, the Spirit said this church was very unfruitful in its service to Him. Jesus says that a tree is known by its fruit, and it was very clear that this church was unfruitful. This church had nothing to show for its efforts as a community based body of believers.

Fifth, the Spirit spoke to me that I would be operating in the nine gifts of the Spirit. Over the years the Spirit has operated in each one of these gifts through me.

Sixth, the Spirit showed me a large screen just ahead of me. On this large screen I was standing beside a large river with a fishing pole in my hand. The river continued to flow past me; then suddenly I cast my line into the river. After about one minute I started catching large gold fish. I had so many of these large gold fish that I could not count them. Then the large screen disappeared, and I was back in the service. After listening to three more songs, I caught a glimpse of something on the right side of the church. This movement excited me very much because it was no one from the congregation. This was a supernatural being of some kind moving very slowly and dressed all in white. Then as I focused in on the image, it was the Holy Ghost that had manifested Himself. I looked upon Him with great joy and excitement as He moved toward the rear of the church. Many people wonder how the Holy Ghost would look. The Holy Ghost looks like a man in every respect, because God said "Let's make man in our image, after our likeness" (Genesis 1:26). The Holy Ghost is God and we are made after his likeness and image. Having seen the Holy Ghost at Christian Unity Church that night started a series of events and manifestations.

Sunday, May 1, 1983 I woke up about 6:00 a.m. for prayer and Bible study. Manifestations of the Holy Ghost had become very frequent. We prepared for church as usual. The only difference was that it was Communion Sunday. For the most part Communion Sunday has historically been very supernatural at Welcome Baptist Church. The communion and the morning worship service were good, but not as great as at other times. During the service this large screen came down from heaven as I stood watching. The Holy Ghost revealed to me an axe head and handle for the axe head. Then the Holy Ghost reminded me of Elisha and the floating axe head. While watching this floating axe head, the Holy Ghost spoke to me. He said, "There is a spy in the camp." He went on to say to me that this person was sent there to watch and disrupt the services. After service was over and we departed for home.

After dinner we attended Trinity Fellowship Church for the evangelistic service. Upon arriving at the church I went straight to the altar to pray. While at the altar I raised my head and hands toward heaven in prayer and praise. With my head and hands raised looking toward heaven, I saw three white doves flying in a circle. I continued to look at these doves for about three to five minutes as they flew around the church. God manifested these three doves right before my eyes. They were real doves. Their feathers were as white as snow.

This was just the beginning of a night that featured this vision. As I got up to leave the altar, I was transported to another place in the spirit. In this place was a large coal furnace and I was shoveling large amounts of coal into the furnace. The fire became very hot and started to blaze out of the door in very large flames. As the evangelistic service was about to start, the Holy Ghost spoke to me that I was going to be like Elisha, the Prophet. Upon hearing this I proceeded to dance all over the church in the spirit of God. I then saw an image of a man walking near the large brown cross in the front of the church. This was the Holy Ghost. I could see the total silhouette of his image and likeness. The Holy Ghost was in the midst of the body of believers. God was in the service with us. Jesus had said, He would send us another comforter. He continued to move around in front of the cross for about five minutes. We continued singing and praising God while my eyes were totally fixed on the Holy Ghost. He then moved past the cross near the choir pews and disappeared from my sight. We had a glorious evangelistic service and it was the first night of revival services.

Many other supernatural things took place. Many were slain in the spirit as the Holy Ghost moved again through the congregation. Some were healed of their afflictions and diseases. For the second time that night I saw the Holy Ghost appear in all white apparel on the right side of the altar. I watched Him as He moved among us. This was another face to face encounter with God, the Holy Ghost. This was another manifestation of His presence that would repeat itself many times.

QUESTIONS FOR GROUP DISCUSSION:

1. What did Paul say concerning "power" in 1 Corinthians 4:20?
2. Constrast this with 1 Corinthians 2:4-5.
3. What hinders churches from being fruitful?

CHAPTER 15

The Miracle of Anna Lee

Do not be afraid, nor be dismayed, for the Lord your God
is with you wherever you go
Joshua 1:9

There are many definitions for the word miracle. Let us look at a few of them. First, a miracle is a work wrought by a divine power for a divine purpose by a means beyond the reach of man. Second, a miracle is an event or effect in the physical world deviating from the known laws of nature, or transcending our knowledge of these laws. Third, a miracle is an extra-ordinary, anomalous, or abnormal event brought about by super-human agency. Fourth, the biblical conception of a miracle is that of some extraordinary work of deity transcending the ordinary powers of nature and wrought in connection with the ends of revelation. The Holy Bible is a miracle book which is replete with miracles, wonders, signs and powers. The Greek word *teras* means wonders. Wonders are supernatural events that leave the state of mind of the eyewitness in wonder by the sight of miracles. The Greek word *semeion* means signs. Signs are seals by which God Himself authenticated the miracle worker. The Greek word *dunamis* means power. When Jesus Christ was baptized by John the Baptist and came up out of the water the heavens opened and the Spirit of God descended on Him like a dove. This

Spirit enabled Him to do miracles, signs and wonders.

The Holy Ghost has worked quite a few miracles at our church. So it was no surprise that the miracle of Anna Lee took place. It was Sunday May 8, 1983. The day started out as every day does with prayer and Bible study around 6:00 a.m. During prayer the spirit gave me the morning worship message which was "God Will Take Care of You." The Spirit also revealed the scriptures that I was to use from 1 Kings 17:9-16. We arrived at church about 10:30 a.m. and noticed a lot of cars parked around the church. There was a large crowd of people. A lot of them were from out of town. Virtually every pew was filled. As we started the service, the Spirit manifested Himself greatly on the congregation and also on me as I preached the word. After the morning message I gave an invitation for people to accept Jesus as their saviour.

The Holy Ghost then commanded me to call sister Anna Lee forward. I had chairs placed in the front facing the congregation and sister Anna Lee sat in one of them. The choir continued to sing as I walked up and down the aisle waiting for the anointing of the Holy Ghost. As I walked toward sister Anna Lee, the choir stopped singing. The deacons stood beside her, and Reverend James Jackson stood with them. I commanded the church to pray along with me. I anointed sister Anna Lee with oil and prayed a small prayer. I asked her if she had any malice, bitterness, and unforgiveness in her heart toward anyone. I asked her if she believed God could heal her, and if she had faith to believe. I asked her if she wanted God to heal her. I then asked her this final question. Did she desire to be healed? To the first question she answered no, but to the others she answered yes.

I laid hands on her, and I began on both knees to pray for God to heal her. The spirit of God spoke to me. While praying for her the spirit of God said, "She is healed." I immediately started jumping on my knees. As the Holy Ghost manifested his power, she began to shout loudly stretching her arms out and kicking her legs straight out. She then jumped off the chair into the air, praising God with a loud voice. The church at this time was praising God and watching with great amazement. Sister Anna Lee had suffered with gout for a number of years. Now she was testifying how God healed her because her legs no longer hurt to walk, the pain was gone and she was able to run the aisle of the church without pain. Her words were, "I feel as good as new" as the church continued to shout and praise God. This was a noticeable miracle because at times sister Anna Lee could not even walk. She would often miss church services for weeks because of the gout in her legs. Many others were blessed and healed that Sunday morning as we continued to praise God with all our hearts.

Later that evening as I left the house to pick up brother Fred Williams. We were going to Trinity Fellowship Church. As I was at the altar I thought about the mighty miracle God performed for sister Anna Lee. I knew that God was about to do something but I had no idea what. The Spirit of God had revealed to me the word of prophecy. Secondly, the Spirit showed me a pyramid with an eye on top of it. Thirdly, the Spirit gave me Joshua 1:6. Then in the middle of the praise and song service a large white screen appeared. It was white like a motion picture screen but very large in size. I was transported to this screen but I did not recognize the surroundings. I was in a foreign country and the people were speaking another language. Then I saw Jesus Christ hanging on the cross with a crown of thorns on his head. Blood was running down his face and dropping on his chest. I could see the nails driven into his hands and feet. Several streams of blood ran from each hand and fell to the ground. Blood also ran from his feet and dropped to the ground. There was blood all over the ground around the cross. Blood, that was as red as crimson, seemed to sparkle as I looked upon it. Then I was transported back to the church to my pew. I looked up and forward. I could see in front of the church an image. This image that I saw revealed the back and front of a person. I saw no face, just a chest dressed all in white with wings. The image seemed to move around on the stage for some minutes and then disappeared. I am convinced this was another manifestation of the Holy Ghost. The miracle of sister Anna Lee, the translation of my spirit, the manifestation of the Holy Ghost made this a remarkable Sunday to say the least.

Questions for Group Discussion:

1. Have you ever experienced a miracle?
2. Do you know anyone who has ever seen a miracle?
3. Compare with Peter's vision in Acts 10:9-18.

CHAPTER

Manifestations and a Miracle

When You said, "Seek My face,"
My heart said to You, "Your face, Lord, I will seek."
Psalm 27:8

The manifestation of the Holy Ghost had been on a very regular basis. The Holy Ghost literally manifested Himself so I could see Him with my naked eye. On June 2, 1983, was the first day of God's chosen fast for me. I ate no food but drank only water. About 1:00 a.m. I was downstairs praying when the Holy Ghost revealed Psalm 27 to me. I had awakened about 6:00 a.m. downstairs praying early that morning I could feel the presence of God in the room. I knew that the Holy Ghost was in the room with me because His presence was so real. Then from nowhere I began seeing white flashes streaking all over the family room. Long white streaks of light that were three to four feet long continuously moved across the room. The presence of the Holy Ghost became very intense. I continued to pray with greater fervor and the presence seemed to greatly grow. I then looked over my left shoulder and saw the image of the Holy Ghost. He was standing directly behind me dressed in a very white garment. This garment was whiter than any garment I had ever seen. I knew this person was the Holy Ghost because I had seen him before. I have often pondered the question. Why has the Holy

Ghost manifested himself to me so often? I have no answer to that question. Only God knows why.

On Sunday, June 12, the eleventh day of the fast, I woke up at 6:00 a.m. and prayed and then I went back to bed. I woke up again at 8:00 a.m., washed and prepared for church. While I was dressing the Holy Ghost spoke to me and said to me, "I'll never let you down." I began to cry intently for a couple of minutes as this was repeated over and over again. Then after I stopped crying I made a promise to God that I would never let Him down in any way. The Holy Ghost gave me the title of that morning's message and the scripture reference. The Holy Ghost said to preach from Luke 6:38 and the title was "If You Don't Have a Lot, Give What You've Got." When we arrived the Holy Ghost's presence was there and God really poured out His spirit during the morning worship. We prayed for the sick and the shut-in and some came to Jesus Christ. After morning services brother Fred Williams and brother Jack Ward had Sunday dinner with us. After dinner we decided we would attend Trinity Fellowship Church for evangelistic services.

Brother Williams and brother Ward and I arrived at the church about 6:30 p.m. and went straight to the altar to pray. I went around greeting all in attendance with handshakes and hugs. We then all burst forth in thunderous praise and song. We sang and praised God for about twenty minutes. I could feel the Holy Ghost's presence in the congregation with the singing and praising. Then as Reverend Jim Mease was in fervor pitch in the song service and praising God with all our might the Holy Ghost spoke to me and revealed to me Isaiah 41:10; Philippians 2:15; and John 1:16. Straight ahead of me toward the stage

I saw long streaks of light that literally lit up the front of the church. After about one minute the streaks of light appeared. Again they lit up the entire front of the stage. These streaks of light had the appearance of lightening. One right after another would streak across the front of the stage near the large brown cross in the rear. These streaks of light were as white as snow and seemed to sparkle as they flashed across the stage.

I was not the only one to see the streaks of light which were three to four feet long. Brother Ward indicated to me that he was watching these same streaks of lights. As we watched these streaks of light continue for about ten minutes the intensity of the Holy Ghost's presence grew stronger and stronger. As we continued to sing and praise God the outline and image of a man-like figure appeared. This image of a man appeared as glowing — dressed in all white garments. This was clearly another manifestation of the Holy Ghost made visible to my eyes. He was standing in the middle of the pews about ten to twelve feet in the air. He was about six feet tall and His raiment shone as the sun as his hair hung to his shoulders. He was floating above the congregation clearly in view as I watched Him. I was absolutely astounded and excited because of His manifested presence. But this time I was not alone as brother Ward saw Him. We looked at each other with great joy and amazement as the Holy Ghost floated above. This manifestation of the Holy Ghost came with streaks of light that looked like lightning. Brother Ward and I continued to look at the Holy Ghost as He moved all around the church. The congregation continued singing and praising God. The Holy Ghost blessed us with His presence. The Holy Ghost just vanished from our eyesight as we had a our eyes fixed on Him. Brother Ward and I continued to look. What a glorious experience to see God manifest Himself to us. That was truly a blessed encounter. I again saw the Holy Ghost face to face in His glory within a matter of days.

On June 19 I completed a seventeen day fast unto God. This fast consisted of water and no food for the entire fast. This next miracle was experienced by a woman in her seventies. I had invited a woman named Mrs. Ann Richards to church many times in the past, but for one reason or another she was unable to attend the services. But on Saturday, June 18 Mrs. Richards telephoned me about attending services. I told her that I would pick her up at her home about 10:30 a.m. Sunday morning. Mrs. Richards had been a good friend of the family for a number of years and often was bedfast and sometimes confined to a wheelchair. Then at other times with the aid of walking canes she could barely walk. The doctors had correctly diagnosed her with rheumatoid arthritis, a crippling disease of the joints. She suffered all the classic symptoms of a persistant inflammation of the joints, marked by atrophy, rarefaction of the bones, and gross deformities. She would suffer agonizing pain for weeks at a time without relief. This Sunday started out as all of the previous ones. I woke up about 6:00 a.m. for prayer and Bible reading. The family was prepared for church and we proceeded to Mrs. Richards's house.

I arrived there about 10:15 a.m. and helped her out of the house. Mrs. Richards was walking with a cane as she was barely able to endure the pain. I put her in the car and we proceeded to the church. She found a place near the front of the church to sit. My father-in-law from Cleveland, Ohio also attended the morning worship service. The morning worship service was glorious as I preached from Luke 7:9-23. The title of the sermon was "Art Thou He That Should Come?" The Holy Ghost was truly in our midst that morning.

After the morning message I gave an invitation for those who wanted to accept Jesus as Saviour. No one came forward; so I asked the deacons to set some chairs up front. The deacons set the chairs up front and I walked back to Mrs. Richards. I helped her from her pew as she walked in great pain to the chairs up front. She sat in one of the chairs with great difficulty in severe pain. She told the congregation of her rheumatoid arthritis and how it had disabled her. I then anointed her with oil and laid my hand on her head and prayed. I prayed that the arthritis would leave her body and never return. She returned to her seat in some pain for the rest of the service. After the service I took her and my father-in-law home.

It was Tuesday, June 21 about 5:50 p.m. when the telephone rang. It was Mrs. Richards. She revealed to me that she had no more pain. She did not need the cane to walk. She revealed that the inflammation had disappeared and she knew that God had performed a miracle. Her doctors told her she was truly healed and that some sort of miracle had taken place. A friend of Mrs. Richards saw her and asked her how was she walking and doing so well. She told the friend that God healed her of rheumatoid arthritis at Welcome Baptist Church on Sunday. We continued to praise God for we knew that God performed this great miracle. The arthritis never came back and Mrs. Richards enjoyed a wonderful life in Jesus. Mrs. Richards was truly healed by the power of God.

QUESTIONS FOR GROUP DISCUSSION:

1. Where do you believe the streaks of light came from?
2. What do you think the streaks of light were?
3. Do you believe everyone can see these images?

CHAPTER 17

Streaks of His Presence

Giving thanks always for all things to God the Father
in the name of our Lord Jesus Christ
Ephesians 5:20

Many people try to explain away the supernatural in this world. God is a supernatural being and there are many realms of the supernatural that man does not understand. People are always trying to use the rationale of their finite mind to understand God. The Bible says that God is beyond understanding. It is impossible for any scientist, inventor, or doctor to ever find out the depths and heights of God's person and character. But man tries and fails every time to secure this knowledge through scientific study. There's only one way to get a clear picture of God and that is through his son Jesus. Jesus Christ is the express image and person of God incarnate in the flesh. There are many supernatural things that are beyond our understanding.

The supernatural experiences that I have witnessed go beyond my ability to understand. The following is a continued series of these supernatural experiences. The day was Saturday, August 27, 1983, a very hot and humid morning. We were preparing to go to Mannington, West Virginia to the funeral of sister Eva Roberts. Sister Roberts had suffered from cancer for a number of years and now God had called her home. Nancy and I left the house and we stopped later to pick up her Aunt Jeannie Bryant. We then arrived at the home of sister Evelyn Smith who accompanied us to the funeral home. But early that morning as I was preparing for the funeral, something got my attention. The room started to light up as if someone was slowly turning up the lights. Then these large flashes of light began streaking through the room. It was like bolts of lightening in the room as they continued to streak across the ceiling above my head. While these large streaks of light danced across the room, I could feel God's mighty presence. Then he appeared — the image of a man about six feet tall wearing a garment that was extremely white but very easy to look upon. He said nothing but only looked at me, and I continued to look upon Him with great reverence. Then after a while he disappeared. These manifestations had started to occur on a very regular basis. I have no idea why the Holy Ghost has continued to manifest himself to me with such regularity. I do feel very blessed that God has chosen me for these visitations.

On Sunday, August 23, 1983 the morning message was from Matthew 7:15-20 entitled, "Beware of False Prophets." We had another glorious service and the Holy Ghost was poured out upon us. After that service I went to Mount Beulah Baptist Church in Grant Town. I was scheduled to preach that afternoon from Matthew 7:15 entitled "Judge Not." We had an enjoyable time in the Lord, but the people were not very responsive. I believe because of the topic of scripture. I left that service and went to Trinity Fellowship

Church. My attention was drawn toward the cross. Suddenly the entire cross and the wall turned very bright with light. I then saw Jesus Christ appear on the cross. This was an absolutely breathtaking site as I focused entirely on Jesus. I had totally forgotten that Reverend Mease was preaching the evening message. I wondered if anyone else could or was seeing what I was seeing. Was this a supernatural manifestation of Jesus exclusively for me? This unbelievable supernatural manifestation lasted for about ten minutes. Then Jesus seemed to have disappeared right off the cross without a trace.

This was not the first time that Jesus had appeared on the cross in this manner. I began to meditate on why Jesus had often manifested Himself to me on the cross. This supernatural manifestation was as real as real could be.

My next experience was one of the most beautiful I have ever seen. It was Sunday, November 20, 1983. I preached and taught with vigor and authority as the Holy Ghost anointed me. The congregation was blessed through the written word of God that morning. At the close of the morning service I departed for Good Hope Baptist Church. At the time for the afternoon message, I saw what appeared to be a bird flying around in the church. This was no ordinary bird. It was very white and glowing as the sun. It flew over the pulpit and all around the inside of the church. The congregation was watching me intently as the Holy Ghost came as a dove. They watched me as I watched this dove fly continuously throughout the congregation. This was the Holy Ghost that had manifested Himself right before my eyes. The church was supercharged with the presence of God.

February 5, 1984, was Communion Sunday at Welcome

Baptist Church. Early that morning many things regarding Ezra were revealed to me in a dream. This Sunday was highlighted by the fact I would dedicate my family to God. After the morning message which was entitled "The immutable God," I dedicated the family. I dedicated them to God because of a vow I made before and after the forty day fast. I vowed to the Lord God that if He let me fast forty days that I would dedicate my family to Him. I successfully completed the forty day fast.

Nancy, my wife and the children, Alethea, Kirsten and Kris Adam, stood before me. I anointed them with oil and dedicated them to God as I promised. The communion service was a glorious one as we gave God the praise and glory. I decided we would attend Trinity Fellowship Church for evening evangelistic service. Reverend Mease preached a message entitled, "What a Spirit-filled Christian Should Be" from Ephesians 5:15-25. While Reverend Mease was preaching I fell into a very deep trance.

In Acts 10:9-10 Peter, while in Joppa, tarried many days with one Simon, a tanner. Peter went up on the housetop to pray about the sixth hour. He then became very hungry and would have eaten but the meal was not ready. Peter fell into trance. A trance is a place or state in which a person has no sensibility to his or her surroundings. Just as Peter had fallen into a trance I also fell into a very deep trance. The first thing I saw was the hand of God. This hand seemed to glisten as the sun, but had no color I have ever seen. Written in the palm of God's hand were these words "My God is with thee." As I focused my eyes the writing in God's hand became very clear. It appeared that the words were burnt into God's hand. The hand seemed to get larger and larger, until the words seemed a foot high.

My thoughts were that this must be the hand of Jesus because of the words "my God." This was a message from God brought to me from Jesus Christ. This was absolutely one incredible experience. But it did not end with this one supernatural experience. I seemed to fall deeper and deeper into the trance. Then I saw Jesus robed in white. He glowed brighter than the sun. His hair lay on his shoulders and He walked toward me with a heavenly smile. He was carrying something—it was a treasure chest full of gold, silver and other precious stones. The outside of this treasure chest, on the sides and top were all manner of jewels. Jesus continued to walk toward me and when he got to me he stopped. As Jesus stood before me with both hands he handed me the treasure chest. The weight of which I could not hold, but had to set it down. I then began to slowly, very slowly depart or come out of this trance. I felt as though I had been out of body. I remember nothing nor remember hearing any of Reverend Mease's message. Was I in my body or was I carried out of my body into this deep trance? The supernatural is a world in which human beings have very little knowledge.

QUESTIONS FOR GROUP DISCUSSION:

1. Why do you think Jesus appeared on the cross?
2. Why do you think the dove appeared?
3. Have you ever fallen into a trance?

CHAPTER 18

Just Like Him

> So God created man in His own image;
> in the image of God He created him;
> male and female He created them.
> Genesis 1:27

We as Christians, should desire to be just like Jesus. Jesus Christ was the expressed image of God the Father. Our greatest desire, as the body of Christ, is to capture the entire essence of God. Many today in Christendom look at God as some natural force to be worshipped. For the most part, ninety per cent of the church really do not know God. They serve Him and worship in the natural instead of in the spirit. Jesus Christ said, "God is a Spirit and they that worship him must worship him in spirit and in truth" (John 4:24). What some people and many Christians do not understand about God is that God is a spirit being, not the sun, stars, moon or some deep voice or force. God is not some man made image of stone, wood, or metal. God is not some thought in the imagination of man with his finite thinking. God is not a man or woman, beast, air, wind, universal mind, or some other uncaring phenomenon. God is a person with an exclusive spirit body, soul and spirit. The difference is that God's body is a spirit and man's body is flesh.

God has been seen bodily many times as stated from the Holy Bible in Genesis 18, 32:24-30; Exodus 24:9-11; Joshua

5:13-15; Isaiah 6; Daniel 7:9-13; Ezekiel 1; Acts 7:56-59 and Revelations 4-5. God can be seen each and every day in the past, present and future. God has been seen with a body, man himself was made in God's image (Genesis 1:26-27). God sat down and ate a meal with Abraham (Genesis 18:8). God wrestled all night with Jacob (Genesis 32:24). Moses saw God face to face out of His glory (Exodus 33:11). Joshua, who was Moses' replacement, and all Israel saw God (Joshua 5:13-15). Samson's parents saw God in bodily form (Judges 13:3-23). The prophet Ezekiel in his writing describes seeing God (Ezekiel 1:26-28; 10:20; 40:3). King David saw Almighty God (1 Chronicles 21:16-17). In the New Testament Stephen saw God and Jesus Christ (Acts 7:56). The apostle John saw and described God in Revelation 4:2-5 and 5:1-7. One day we shall all see God (Revelations 21:3-4; 22:4). God is not some natural being, but is a supernatural spirit being. The church should see God as a supernatural being that should be worshipped in spirit and in truth.

The next supernatural experience that was manifested to me was glorious and humbling. On Sunday, February 12, 1984, the morning message was from Hebrews 11:6, entitled "It's Impossible to Please God Without Faith." Many were blessed and we prayed for many who had problems and God delivered them. During this time in my ministry God was leading me more and more into the supernatural. I was pastoring a Baptist church but often attending a Pentecostal Full Gospel church.

While attending an evangelistic service the Holy Ghost

spoke to me with this message, "You're on the move." I was transported spiritually before Jesus as he hung on the cross. As I stood there before Christ a sword appeared and it cut him on the right side. A large amount of blood and water gushed from his side which flowed to the ground. I stood there in utter amazement. I was spiritually detached from the church service. Then one of the most unusual supernatural things took place. I was standing under a waterfall with tons of water coming down on me. Then I was instantly dressed in a long white robe as the water continued to pour on me. The water felt spiritually soothing, and then as from nowhere Jesus appeared standing directly in front of me. It was Jesus and yet it was me. I was looking at Jesus but it was me. I was one with Jesus. The water continued to flow over me and Jesus in large torrents of velocity and turbulence. Then this long brown hair from the head of Jesus appeared to me. As the water continued to fall on me from this large waterfall, my entire body had a very bright gold glow around it. The water continued to fall in large torrents as I looked at Jesus and he looked at me. Then I moved from the waterfall and suddenly I was in a country I did not recognize. As I stood there looking, my hands were literally flames of fire. The flames of fire came off my hands about four inches but it did not burn. There was no pain involved at all and my hands took on a reddish blue color. Then I looked down and my feet were ablaze as flames of fire came off of them. My feet and hands blazed with fire, yet there was no pain or damage to them.

As my hands and feet were ablaze with fire, I noticed a crown on my head. It was as though I was looking into a mirror. A bright and shiny crown adorned the top of my head which was full of precious stones. I saw Jesus walking toward me holding something in his hands. As He came closer I could see it was a gold seal. As Jesus stood in front of me, he very slowly handed the gold seal to me. I clutched it in my hands as to never drop it or lose it. Suddenly I was back in my body as being transported as fast as the speed of light. Where was I and where had I gone for an hour? What outer dimension was I translated to for an hour? As Reverend Mease started the evening message I had no recollection of the praise and worship service. Being transported spiritually has been a very common occurrence in my ministry.

My next supernatural experience took place on Sunday, March 11, 1984. As I started through the front door of the church I could feel the power of God as I continued to walk toward the altar to pray, I saw something. As I was half way down the aisle a large movie screen dropped down in front of me. I saw a man wearing garments from Old Testament times. His clothes seemed to me tattered and somewhat wrinkled. He had a beard and looked to be about fifty to sixty years old. The man had no color as he was neither black or white. He appeared to be about six feet tall with grayish looking long hair. I then saw an axe, but there was no one holding the axe. It appeared as though it was suspended in mid air above the man's head. The axe seemed to hover above the man's head for a matter minutes. Then the axe seemed to move down toward the top of the man's head. Then with a quick burst it struck the man in the top of the his head. But the axe did not stop there it continued down through the man's body. The man appeared in two pieces as I stood there in the middle of the church. One miraculous thing took place, there was no blood as I saw the man cut in half. Then I heard these words spoken in an audible voice, "The axe must fall." I stood there thinking and musing at great length the significance of this great vision. Then the man disappeared and a bow and arrow drawn back replaced the ax. This drawn bow remained on the large picture screen for about a minute. It also vanished off the screen very slowly. The entire large picture screen also vanished in a moment. I walked slowly toward the altar and kneeled down at the altar and prayed before sitting down.

I then saw myself with long white wings. These wings hung down from my back and I could see them clearly. These long white wings appeared to be made from feathers but they did not feel like feathers to the touch of my hands. These supernatural experiences started very early in my Christian life. They continued on all throughout my walk with Jesus. I cannot explain why they happen with such frequency and intensity. Praise God to the highest.

Questions for Group Discussion:

1. Has God ever manifested Himself to you?
2. What meaning does the waterfall have?
3. What does the axe mean? Compare with 1 Kings 18:17-40.

CHAPTER

Smoke, Fire, Oil, and Wings

Ask, and it will be given to you; seek, and you will find; knock, and it will be opened to you.
Matthew 7:7

The Holy Bible in itself is a supernatural book with many supernatural occurrences found within its covers. Many men and women have experienced the awesome nature of God in the realm of the supernatural. Many scholars try to explain away the miracles and supernatural events of the Bible. The mystery of God far exceeds man's ability to reason with the supernatural. The realm of God and the supernatural operate, function, and exist on another plane. God is a Spirit, thus, He operates on a supernatural level in the realm of the spirit, although He does and can manifest himself in the natural world so that men and women can see these manifestations, demonstrated on a level they can sometimes understand.

The following experiences demonstrate God's omnipotence and willingness to reveal the supernatural to mankind. On Saturday, June 30, 1984. the day started out as all my days do with early morning prayer. Nancy told me previously that some of her friends might stop in that day. We waited with some expectation for their arrival that Saturday morning. Nancy worked with these friends of hers at the lamp plant in Fairmont. They are Christians who love God. Nancy had spoken of them many times. It was about 10:00 a.m. when her friends arrived. We talked for about ten minutes and then sang songs for about twenty minutes. The power of the Holy Ghost came upon her friend and she started speaking in an unknown tongue. Her friend danced and sang in the spirit and was then slain in the spirit. The house appeared to fill with a blue smoke. We all had difficulty standing as the blue smoke seemed to get thicker and thicker. The Lord God really blessed us that Saturday morning. This was the second time that this blue smoke filled the entire house. This would not be the last time that this particular supernatural phenomenon would take place.

One of the most spectacular supernatural visions took place on July 1, 1984. That morning I was invited to Mount Pleasant Baptist Church to bring the message. The morning text was from 1 John 3:20-25. The Holy Ghost had given this scripture in a dream. In the same dream the voice of God spoke to me. God said, "If you want to learn more of Jesus Christ read 1 John 2." That morning at Mount Pleasant church we had a glorious time and we prayed for many and our prayers were answered.

Later that afternoon we decided to go to Trinity Fellowship Church were I have been increasingly led to go. The supernatural manifestations of God had increased dramatically since I started attending the evening services. This particular Sunday was no different. The presence of God was so strong that I was one hundred percent sure that God was about to do something glorious. During the message on evangelism, I felt as if I was about to leave my body. Then it happened in a moment of a twinkling of an eye, I was gone. A large picture screen appeared before me and I was carried to this large theater. I could not identify with any certainty. The surroundings of this theater. I was in a strange place where I recognized nothing and no one. Thoughts raced through my spirit; where was I? How did I get here and who was I going to see? I continued to reason, why was I brought to this theater and for what purpose? Then what seemed to be in a short time, something amazing appeared in the foreground. I stood there in total amazement as what appeared to be fire flying toward me. As this fire, which was blue-red in color, came toward me I felt no fear. As the fire drew nearer and nearer there appeared tongs with fire in them. Then as the tongs came closer and closer I was frozen with amazement. Then as the tongs filled with fire came directly in front of me my mouth opened. My tongue very slowly protruded out as far as it would go. Then the tongs filled with fire came and dropped a hot coal of fire on my tongue. It did not burn or hurt. I did not really have a feeling at all. It just sat there on my tongue and seemed to blaze higher and higher. These tongs seemed to have disappeared and my tongue still felt no effects of this burning coal. I stood there still in utter amazement at what was taking place. Then my mouth closed with this burning hot coal still on my tongue. I cannot remember if I swallowed the hot burning coal or if it remained on my tongue. This separation lasted for an undetermined amount of time for when I returned I could remember nothing of the message. How long was I gone and where did I go? But more importantly, what was the significance of the tongs placing the burning coal on my tongue? I thought again and again what was the immediate and long term significance of this experience?

 The next great supernatural experience took place on

Sunday, July 15, 1984. I brought the message from Matthew 7:7-8 as the Lord anointed me with great power. I again laid hands on the sick and prayed for many other needs of the people. The morning service ended on a glorious high note of songs and praise to God. That evening I was led by the spirit to attend Trinity Fellowship Church. I felt deep in my soul that God had been leading me to attend these services on a regular basis. The Holy Spirit revealed to me one of the most glorious things I had ever seen. As I was up around the altar the heavens opened and I saw myself in another world. I was standing all alone with no one around me. The room was all white, the floor, the walls, and the ceiling. The most unusual aspect of this all white room was that it had no furniture in it. There were no windows or doors and even more astounding there were no seams or lines on anything. A perfectly square, white room with no lines, doors or windows. I appeared standing in the middle of this all white room. My hands were cupped together as I stood straight up in the room. Suddenly a large stream of oil flowed in my hands from above. The most incredible thing about this was the oil did not come from a pitcher or vessel of any kind. It flowed down out of mid air straight into my hands filling them up. Then the oil overflowed my hands and started falling to the all white floor below. This continued for the space of an undetermined amount of time. The oil continued to flow from mid air into my hands. I stood there in total amazement as the floor now was beginning to be covered with the oil. It fell from my hands to the ground and now had completely covered the floor and my feet.

  Then I was transported back to the altar where I was standing in prayer and praise. Almost immediately I saw in the front of the church near the cross a series of lights. These flashes of light in streaks of six to ten feet long engulfed the church. They moved across the front and the rear of the church as in concert with one another. I have seen these lights before but never to such degree of movement. What did it all mean? What was the purpose of the all white room and the oil that flowed from mid air? What did the lights mean that streaked across the church? Was God manifesting the supernatural power of His divine purpose? If so, why to me in this manner?

The next great manifestation took place on August 19, 1984, Sunday evening. The place was Trinity Fellowship Church for evening service. The service was about half way through when I felt myself somewhat detached from my body. I was carried to a place I could not recognize. I saw no one else there but I did not feel that I was alone. It felt as though I was in a room with many people yet I neither saw nor heard any one speak or move. Then as the presence of God seemed to greatly grow in this room I looked down and saw what appeared to be wings. These wings were not made of feathers, but took on the appearance of feathers. They were attached to my back. One on either side of my upper back. They hung almost to the ground with large feather like grooves. The wings were very large, but I could not feel them as they hung down from my back. Then a voice said, "These are the wings of healing." I thought to myself the wings of healing were attached to my back. What did all this mean and how was God going to use me in this ministry?

The wings felt and looked so real as I stood there in this large room. Did the wings have a significance? If they did, what did that mean for me? I was drawn back, back and finally realized I was in my body again.

QUESTIONS FOR GROUP DISCUSSION:

1. Have you ever seen mysterious smoke?
2. Have you ever had an out of body experience?
3. Do you know someone who has had supernatural experiences?

CHAPTER

Jesus Appears to Me

Mary Magdalene came and told the disciples that she had seen the
Lord, and that He had spoken these things to her.
John 20:18

Jesus had been crucified, entombed and rose again on the third day. Jesus appeared to Mary Magdalene (John 20:11-18). Mary stood outside the sepulchre weeping, and as she wept, she stooped down and looked into the sepulchre. Mary saw two angels in white sitting, the one at the head and the other at the feet where the body of Jesus had lain. The angels spoke to Mary and said unto her, "Woman, why weepest thou?" Mary's response was, "Because they have taken away my Lord, and I know not where they have laid Him." Mary probably thought someone had stolen the body of Jesus to hide it. Mary turned back around and saw Jesus standing there, but she did not recognize Him. No one really knows why Mary was not able to recognize that it was Jesus. Jesus spoke to Mary, "Woman, why weepest thou? Whom seekest thou?" Mary thought that Jesus was the gardener. Then she replied, "Sir, if thou have borne Him hence, tell me where thou has laid Him. I will take Him away." Jesus knew who Mary was seeking, but He let her respond to His questions anyway. Jesus then called her by name, "Mary." She then turned and said to Jesus "Rabboni" which means, Master. She then recognized Jesus. She was the first person to whom He revealed himself. She was also the first person to shout abroad that He was risen. Jesus said to Mary "touch me not for I am not yet ascended to my father but go and tell my brethren." He told Mary to "go tell the brethren I ascend unto My Father, and your Father and to My God, and to your God." Jesus did not want Mary to hold Him because He was on his way to heaven. Jesus ascended to heaven and then returned to meet with His brethren as He promised.

In verse 18 Mary Magdalene gave her testimony of the resurrection. Mary came to the disciples and told them that she had seen the Lord. He had spoken these things unto her near the sepulchre. But the disciples in fear and trembling did not believe Mary's testimony of Jesus. In John 20:19-20 Jesus appeared to the disciples, but Thomas was missing. Jesus having ascended to the Father in Heaven, returned at evening time. It was the first day of the week, and the disciples had the doors closed in fear of the Jews. Where was Thomas? Was he not also afraid of the Jews? Then one of the most spectacular miracles took place, Jesus came and stood in the midst. This miracle must have really startled the disciples. One moment the disciples were in a room by themselves, and the next Jesus stood in their midst. Jesus said to them to quiet their fears, "Peace be unto you." Jesus had a resurrected body. He needed no door to enter into the house. In this body Jesus had the ability to appear and disappear. To put it another way to be visible or invisible at His will. Jesus then showed His disciples His hands and His side. Upon doing this the disciples were glad. They rejoiced when they saw it was Him, whose hands had been nailed. The one who had been pierced in His right side was again with them.

❖

On Sunday, October 14, 1984, one of the most glorious miracles took place in my home. This particular Sunday was no different from any other except that I was not pastoring a church. I had resigned from Welcome Baptist Church to attend Trinity Fellowship Church Full Gospel. I was encouraged by the Holy Ghost to resign, because my spiritual growth had ceased to increase there. I attended Trinity Fellowship for evening evangelistic services. The Reverend Odie Herron preached about the Ten Commandments in our lives everyday. The service was a glorious one and I continued to praise God when I arrived home that night. This was the fourth day of a fast that consisted of just water and no food. Later on that night I wrote in my daily journal about all of Sunday's events.

As I sat on the bed writing in my journal the presence of God became more intense. The presence and power of God filled my entire bedroom. I felt as if God was in the bedroom with me. His presence was very strong. Having finished writing in my journal, I got on my knees in prayer. After about ten minutes of prayer, I could feel the presence of someone behind me. This had happened many times before, so I really did not expect anything to happen. I continued to pray for about five minutes more then the presence manifested himself. I looked over my right shoulder and glimpsed at what appeared to be a person. I then stopped praying and turned around completely to get a better look at this person. It was Jesus in the flesh. This was no vision. I was not out of my body. I was not transported somewhere else as at other times. I was in my bedroom on my knees with Jesus standing directly in front of me. He wore a white robe that shone like the sun in brightness. He stood about six feet tall with brown hair down to his shoulders. He had brown eyes and wore a beard short in length. The complexion of Jesus was olive brown with no imperfections. I remained on my knees for one or two minutes then Jesus moved toward me. Jesus raised His right hand, put it on my left shoulder. He then removed His right hand, raised it then put it on the top of my head. I thought this was absolutely incredible. Would anybody believe me when I told them? Jesus had appeared to Mary Magdalene and some of the disciples doubted her. Now Jesus had appeared to me in His glorified flesh and bone body.

Jesus' right hand remained on the top of my head for about thirty seconds. Then He raised it, took two steps backwards and vanished. He literally vanished as I gazed upon Him. This was one of the most incredible supernatural experiences I ever witnessed. This without a doubt was Jesus Christ the Son of God that appeared in my bedroom.

Then in just four days, I would see Jesus as He appeared to me again. This face to face meeting with Jesus in my bedroom would only be the beginning of many. This next meeting with Jesus took place on October 18 early in the morning. Jesus' appearance to me this time was different because He appeared in a dream. The first dream consisted of Reverend James Jackson, a good friend, discussing the end times of the Bible. He had some questions, so we talked about these matters for a time. In the second dream, I saw some scriptures from the Bible. They just appeared before my eyes moving from left to right. Then I saw Jesus dressed in a long white robe. The robe was white and glistened with brightness. Jesus was sitting on a stool, clutching close to His bosom what appeared to be books. As I moved closer and closer to Him it was not books at all but two tablets. Jesus was holding two tablets close to His bosom. I could not read what was written upon these two tablets. I looked Jesus in the face. It was surely Him as He appeared to me in my bedroom. Within the space of four days Jesus had appeared first in my bedroom and now in this dream. The Jesus that had appeared to me in flesh and bone was the same Jesus that appeared to me in the dream. This started a series of dreams, visions, and other manifestations that only grew in intensity.

QUESTIONS FOR GROUP DISCUSSION:

1. How would you describe Jesus' glorified body?
2. Have supernatural beings ever appeared in your dreams?
3. Compare with Matthew 1:18-25.

CHAPTER 21

Heat, Wind, and Jesus

Blessed is the glory of the Lord from His place!
Ezikiel 3:12

The word heat has many meanings of which I'll give a few. The first, of which we are all familiar with, heat is associated with being hot. Heat or excessive heat causes the temperature to rise. The second, heat is associated with warmth, which may heat a building, room or a house. The third, heat is associated with the soul of man. Heat here means or involves great intensity or passion of feeling for something or someone. The prophet Ezekiel in his second vision of glory was taken up and transported to another place. In Ezekiel 3:12-16 the prophet is caught up by the spirit and transported but where was he transported to and for what reason? Ezekiel had been commissioned three times by God to go to Israel. In verse 12 the spirit took him up and carried him away to the captives along the river Chebar. As all this was taking place, Ezekiel said he heard a voice behind him as of a great rushing, which spoke these words unto him,"Blessed be the glory of the Lord from his place." Was the voice the voice of God or an angel? As Ezekiel was in flight to the river Chebar, he heard some additional noise. In verse 13 the prophet said he heard the noise of wings. These wings belonged to the living creatures that touched one another. The prophet then heard the noise of wheels that were over against them. And again the prophet heard the noise of a great rushing. This great rushing noise was the voice of the cherubim. In verse 13 Ezekiel said, "the spirit lifted me up and took me away." What Ezekiel was saying was that he was literally taken by the spirit in the flesh. This was not a vision or a dream but he was literally being carried in the flesh and blood. The Bible also records others who have been carried away in the flesh. The apostle John in Revelations 1:10 and Revelation 4:1 was carried into heaven. Ezekiel says he went in the bitterness and in the heat of his spirit. The prophet was very upset with the people of Israel. But why was he so bitter with Israel? It was their spiritual condition that so angered him. The people of Israel were spiritually destitute and yet they rejected God and his message. Ezekiel demonstrated in the heat of his spirit, a righteous indignation for the sins that Israel were committing. Then Ezekiel says, "but the hand of the Lord was strong upon me." What the prophet was essentially saying was that God Almighty was there to supernaturally strengthened him for his commission.

It was November 4, 1984, Sunday evening at Trinity Fellowship Church. What I'm about to tell you was one of the most unusual supernatural occurrences I have ever experienced. This particular evangelistic service was no different from any other service. The message was from John 10:4-5 entitled, "What Kind of Voices do we Hear or Obey?" After the message was preached, people were called to the altar. Everyone in attendance came to the altar for prayer and praise. Some were singing, some were praising God and some worshipped God in total silence.

I came to the altar and prayed for those who desired or who were seeking God. I returned to the altar and prayed and praised with uplifted hands toward God. As my hands were raised toward heaven I felt some heat on my forehead. The heat grew in intensity and I began to sweat profusely. Large drops of sweat appeared on my head and face. Sweat ran down my face from my forehead in large streams. My entire body was soon completely wet with sweat from this very intense heat. I used a handkerchief that I had with me, and it was soon all wet also. The handkerchief had soaked up so much sweat that I was able to wring it out. This enormous heat then encircled my body as if I was in the middle of a ring of heat. This ring of heat moved in a clockwise motion around me. This even created more and more heat as I was still praying and praising God. I would occasionally wipe away the sweat that got into my eyes. My shirt and tie were completely wet. My suit looked as if I jumped into a swimming pool. There was not one dry place on my body. I continued praying and praising as the heat that encircled me continued to magnify. I could sense the presence of a person during this entire experience. The circle became tighter and tighter as I felt the glory of God envelop me. I continued earnestly in prayer, praise and worship as the presence of God engulfed me. This lasted for about twenty minutes then the circle of heat that engulfed me disappeared. It started to move upward over my shoulders and then my head. It continued to move toward the ceiling until it reached the ceiling were it disappeared. I returned to my seat wet from my head to my toes.

One of the most interesting things happened to me as I returned to my seat. As I sat there in my seat, a very soft wind blew on me. I looked around to see if a window was open or the overhead fans were on. There were no windows open, neither were there any fans on. What was this wind that constantly blew upon me during the evening service? I cannot explain the origin of this wind. It seemed to blow from all directions at once. Where did these winds or wind come from? Was I the only one in the church to experience these supernatural winds. This was the first time that this kind of supernatural experience took place. Were these winds from God? Was the Holy Ghost manifesting himself in some new way? The winds continued to blow upon me the entire evangelistic service even as we dismissed for the night.

On Wednesday, March 13, 1985 four days from my birthday, was the beginning of a three day fast that consisted of no food or water. During the fast I prayed for some things in particular. One of which was a world wide revival. This day was earmarked by a lot of praying, praising and worshipping God. Later on in the afternoon I took a short nap. While asleep I dreamed I was standing in what appeared to be a clearing in the midst of a lot of trees. There was grass under my feet and the sun shone brightly in the sky. There appeared to be a little speck or black spot off in the distance. As I looked up in the sky this speck or black spot drew closer and closer. I could see now it was Jesus dressed completely in a long white robe. This robe sparkled with brightness and beauty as he hovered just in the tree tops. He continued to descend until He was almost on the ground where I stood. I continued to look upon Jesus without saying a word. He continued to look at me with a joyous smile. Then suddenly he ascended back into the heavens. Why did Jesus come and visit me?

What purpose did he have in mind with this supernatural visitation? I was never able to answer these questions to my fullest satisfaction.

Questions for Group Discussion:

1. Have you ever been transported to another place?
2. Have you ever experienced any feelings of supernatural heat?
3. How would you describe the circle of heat?

CHAPTER

God in the Hands of Man

Let this mind be in you which was also in Christ Jesus
Philippians 2:5

Christians in the world today have reduced the omnipotent God to an impersonal force. They have turned the truth of God into a lie. A large segment of the church has changed the supernatural God into a natural God. A natural God who has isolated himself in heaven from the perils and evils of this world and has limited power to change lives and world affairs. Of course none of this is true. God has not changed but many Christians have. God cannot change because He is immutable, and man does not possess this divine attribute. Many Christians are blown to and fro by every wind of doctrine. Many Christians today can be considered very double minded in all their ways.

But God wants to put himself in the lives of Christians. Christians can obtain power in the days of the dispensation of the Holy Ghost. How can Christians obtain the power of God? The question is a very simple one to answer. First, the almighty commanding power of Christ can be in you with the use of His name and the indwelling Holy Ghost. Second, it is the Holy Ghost that speaks the things of the Father. Through your born again experience with Christ he has been formed in you and He is becoming complete in you. The Christian church will never totally fulfill its worldwide mission until it has been endued with Pentecostal power. I could repeat this over and over hundreds of times. Most of the Christians in church today are just playing church. A great number of Christians are spiritual vampires. They look in the mirror, and instead of seeing Christ they see no image at all. Christians are suppose to be just like Christ, but many are spiritual vampires. If Christians are to win the world for Christ, it must be empowered by spiritual gifts. The modern day church must encounter a spiritual awakening. This will only happen if the church gets spirit filled and be led by the Holy Ghost. We cannot stress enough that the church needs to revisit Pentecost. Christians that have been baptized in the Holy Ghost have the power and gifts in them. They are not just merely manifested through them as some think. As born again believers, baptized in the Holy Ghost, we are partakers of His nature. And most importantly we have the divine life of God dwelling in us. Christians must thoroughly realize that we are God's dwelling place. The statements just mentioned should always ring true in our hearts. We need to be endued with power. I must repeat this as often as possible. The gifts of the spirit are resident in every born again believer who has been baptized in the Holy Ghost. Whenever we pray, fast, and are led by the Holy Ghost, then these gifts will be manifested. I'll mention this one more time for my readers. The gifts of the spirit are resident in those who are born again, and are baptized in the Holy Ghost with the evidence of speaking in an unknown tongue.

For many years I prayed that God would use me in a way that He would receive the glory. The next supernatural experience took place on Sunday, April 21, 1985. This experience started what was to be the beginning of many similar ones. Since God is in you, God in effect is in our hands. God is in the hands of man and this supernatural experience started my ministry of praying for the sick in real earnest.

On April 18, 1985, I was praying downstairs in the family room. It was early in the morning about 6:00 a.m. that I began to pray in earnest. During the course of praying, praising and worshipping God He revealed this message to me. The spirit said and I quote, "You will have a heavenly visitation." I was not startled at the message or even surprised because I have had many visitations. What did surprise me was that the Spirit was telling me in advance. With the other heavenly visitations, the Holy Ghost, would just appear without any warning. On Sunday, April 21 I preached from Philippians 2:1-5, and the Lord God really blessed the message. It was a very powerful message. The congregation was very responsive to the message and it touched their hearts. The Holy Ghost prepared their hearts to receive a blessing. At the end of the message I gave an altar call. One man gave his life to Christ to be his savior. Many who were in a backslidden state came and repented of their sins. God healed many for whom we prayed.

I attended the evening service and preached from Psalm 136. The Lord God really blessed us in a mighty way with healings and some supernatural occurrences. That night I was praying downstairs in the family room. This prayer was quite different in that the mighty presence of God Almighty was there. The presence of God Almighty was so real that I felt He was actually in the room. I sensed and felt a real presence of Him. As I continued to pray in earnest, something most supernaturally unusual took place.

There appeared over my head a flashing white light that was as bright as the sun. This light continued to blink off and on as if it were being controlled by God. Then I felt an intense heat in my right foot. This intense heat burned my right foot, but not to leave scars or marks. Then with a great rush of heavenly power I was slain in the spirit. I fell backward on the bed and lay there motionless. I felt a peace and joy such as I have never known. Everything was white but somewhat smoky in this state of unconsciousness under the power of God. Then I heard a voice say unto me, "the left hand would have the power in it." I was being told that the power of God at His command would flow through my left hand.

While slain in the spirit I asked the Lord God for "miracles, healings and anointed words." I continued to ask the Lord God for "anointed services at the revival this week." Monday night, May 13 I was engrossed in earnest fervent prayer. Someone put his hand on my shoulder. I knew it was God because that was not the first time this had taken place. I could feel His presence, His divine presence like the image of a man. His hand rested on my shoulder as I continued to walk back and forth in prayer.

I also attended Trinity Fellowship church for evening services. I preached from 1 John 5:13-15. It was an anointed message and service. The service was highlighted by sister Anna Johnson being healed. She described it to me this way. As I was preaching a very warm and intense heat started at her head and soon was all over her body. She had been suffering from throat and chest problems. This intense heat which covered her entire body completely healed her of these problems. We had been praying for about a week for sister Johnson and now God has healed her.

QUESTIONS FOR GROUP DISCUSSION:

1. Are you letting God use you?
2. How do you feel about being slain in the Spirit?
3. How would you describe the state of today's church?

CHAPTER

The Holy Ghost Like a Dove

And the Holy Spirit descended in bodily form
like a dove upon Him
Luke 3:22

Before Jesus started his public ministry some startling supernatural events took place. John the Baptist in Luke 3:16 made an extraordinary prediction about Jesus. The people were in expectation and mused in their hearts as to whether he was Christ or not. There must have been a lot of suspense and drama as the people debated in their hearts whether he was the long awaited Messiah. John answered the people saying, "I indeed baptize you with water: but one mightier than I cometh, the latchet of whose shoes I am not worthy to unloose: he shall baptize you with the Holy Ghost and with fire." John knew that there was a physical baptism in water, but he also knew there was a spiritual baptism. John acknowledged Jesus as the Messiah, the Son of God. John said he was not worthy to unloose his shoes. What did John mean when he made that statement?

The shoes of that time were only soles with strings or possibly thongs which tied around the feet. Unloosening the shoes was seen as a mark of great respect for a disciple of their master. Even John felt unworthy of such a great honor as this. John continued by saying, "he shall baptize you with the Holy Ghost and fire." We know this was fulfilled on the day of Pentecost in Acts 2:1-4.

In Jesus' final preparation for his ministry as seen in Luke 3:21-22 some remarkable things took place. Many people had come to John, heard the word and were baptized in water. It came to pass that Jesus, as He was being baptized and praying, the heaven opened. God set the stage that Jesus should be baptized last and that all around should see His baptism. The only reason Christ was baptized in water was to illustrate his death, burial and resurrection. The next thing we see is Jesus praying and the heavens were opened. The heavens will open up for those like Jesus who are willing to take the time to pray. In the Bible there is recorded where six men saw the heavens open up. Ezekiel in Ezekiel 1:1, Jesus in Mark 1:10, Nathanael in John 1:51, Stephen in Acts 7:56, Peter in Acts 10:11, and John in Revelations 4:1; 11:19; 19:11.

When Jesus saw the heavens open up there appeared to be a white bird of some kind descending from heaven. But wait, it was more than just a bird, it was the Holy Ghost in bodily shape. Luke 3:22 describes the account in great detail of Jesus' spirit baptism. Luke said the Holy Ghost descended in a bodily shape like a dove upon Jesus, and a voice from heaven said, "Thou art my beloved Son; in thee I am well pleased." Now the Holy Ghost is not a dove but descended like a dove from Heaven. This was a symbol that Jesus' mission would be one of peace and love. God the Father left no doubt in the minds of men forever with his statement. "Thou art my beloved Son; in thee I am well pleased." I must repeat that the Holy Ghost is not a dove, but came down in the bodily shape of a dove. God's ways are very mystifying at times and this incident of Jesus fits into that category. We know that the Holy Ghost is a person but God decided that He would come in the bodily shape of a dove. God's ways are beyond knowing, so it is very futile for us to try.

Tuesday, July 9, 1985 will go down as one of the most mystical experiences I ever had. In the same way that Jesus was baptized in water and then by the Holy Spirit coming in the bodily shape of a dove, I also encountered the Holy Ghost in the bodily shape of a dove. The following account is word for word as I wrote it down after the experience.

> *I was dissatisfied and very unhappy about the way God was handling some things in the ministry as well as in my personal life. I complained to God about always preaching in these small churches and not receiving the promise He made to me some years ago. I was walking on the right side wall facing the pulpit near the second or middle window. This window was partially open to the width of a very small crack. As I was walking toward the front praying and complaining to God about my situation I could see a bird flying at a very swift speed. But this was not a regular bird. The color was a whitish-gray. This bird was small in size, but not a very small bird like a sparrow. As I was praying I could see this bird over my left shoulder. This bird was flying directly toward me and as it flew closer it startled me. As it got about a foot away from me I threw up both my hands. Then I quickly put down both my hands as I thought maybe the bird would fly directly into my face.*
>
> *What I thought was a bird was in fact the Holy Ghost in the bodily shape of a dove. While my hands were raised*

the dove flew right into my hands. I could see this whitish gray bird enter into my hands penetrating them. It happened so fast that maybe the dove flew by my hands. But I'm sure he entered them and never came out the other side. I thought maybe I imagined the whole thing so I started looking for the dove. I looked for the dove in the ceiling and down on the floor. I searched in the curtains which surrounded the windows. I searched for one hour trying to find this mysterious dove. The only lights that were on in the building were the spot lights pointed straight down. Only these lights were on and the light that came through the windows of the church. The church was somewhat dark. I went to the back of the church and switched on all the lights in the sanctuary. I then went back to the middle window and I saw no sign of the dove. The windows on the right side of the sanctuary were all open a little. But the dove could not have flown out of these windows, especially the middle one. It only had a crack for an opening. I continued to look for the dove, then I gave up the search and turned off the lights in the sanctuary. As I was preparing to leave the church I heard these words, "It was the Holy Spirit."

This voice resonated all through my body with great vibrations. I then said to myself if it was the Holy Spirit I would and should see a change take place. Almost immediately upon saying this I began to feel strange from the top of my head to the soles of my feet. This strange feeling felt like a great earthquake with shaking and great physical gyrations. I know for a absolute fact the dove was the Holy Ghost. I know for an absolute truth that he flew into and penetrated the flesh of my hands. God the Holy Ghost flew directly into my hands and remained there. This was *without a doubt the most unusual feeling I ever received and experienced.*

Just as this experience was one of the greatest I ever witnessed there would be many more in the days to come that would rival it.

QUESTIONS FOR GROUP DISCUSSION:

1. Why did the Holy Ghost come in the form of a dove?
2. Contrast with Matthew 3:13-17.
3. What encounters have you had with the Holy Ghost?

CHAPTER

The Miracle of the Oil

But seek first the kingdom of God and His righteousness,
and all these things shall be added to you.
Matthew 6:33

The prophet Elisha worked mighty miracles in the land of Israel. Elisha worked a great miracle when he multiplied the widow's oil. The account of this great miracle is in 2 Kings 4:1-7. Many consider this as Elisha's seventh miracle in the string of his many miracles.

There was a certain woman who was married to a prophet who served God with gladness and fear. She came to Elisha asking for help because her husband was dead. She told Elisha that the creditor was coming to take her two sons away and that the creditor would make them bondmen or slaves. Her husband left his wife no large sum of money. His creditors wanted their money and they were persuaded to take her two sons as bondmen. The woman came to Elisha who was head man of the schools of the prophets and asked him for help. The law of Moses gave the creditors the right to claim the two sons of the debtor who was unable to pay. The two sons would serve or work for the creditors until the year of Jubilee or after seven years. Then after Jubilee they would be free or released back to their mother. The scriptures state this many times in the following references, Leviticus 25:30-41; Nehemiah

5:5-8 and Job 24:9.

Elisha then asked the woman two questions. "What shall I do for thee?" Then he asked her another question. "Tell me what has thou in the house?" She responded by answering the second question and not the first. She said she did not have anything in the house, except a pot of oil. She had a flask of oil that many historians believe was an earthen vessel. It had a sharp bottom which was deep and narrow. Possibly it might have been made of metal also. Then Elisha told the woman to go borrow some empty vessels from all her neighbors, and not a few. This was a command from Elisha to the woman. Would she obey the man of God? Would she ask him many questions as to why? The woman and her sons went to all her neighbors and borrowed many vessels. Did the woman ever think when she might ever have enough? Was enough sufficient for her and her sons when they were finished borrowing vessels? Then the prophet told her to shut the door. When she came into her house she and her sons started pouring out the oil. What faith the woman and the sons must have displayed in obeying Elisha's command. She took the pot of oil she had. Her sons lined up the empty vessels then she started to pour. She filled up the first vessel, then the second, and then the third. The woman must have been totally amazed at the miracle that she and her sons were witnessing. She continued to pour one right after the other maybe in fear it would fail. Maybe she continued to pour with total confidence as to the word of Elisha. At any rate she set aside all the full vessels and continued to pour until all the vessels were full. She then asked for another vessel and her one son said to her, "there is not a vessel more." The oil which was in the woman's pot stayed completely full as at the beginning. The woman went and told Elisha the man of God what took place. Then Elisha said to her, "Go sell the oil and pay your debts." She and her sons could live from the rest. The woman obeyed every command of Elisha and demonstrated great faith in his word. The woman prospered because she first came to Elisha and second she demonstrated faith and obedience. God had a miracle for this woman because she sought the man of God first.

Jesus said in Matthew 6:33, "But seek ye first the kingdom of God and His righteousness and these things shall be added unto you." In times of distress if we seek God first, he will multiply our oil and give us a miracle also.

On February 1, 1987 I experienced a very notable miracle. Before the morning service I went to my clothes closet. I selected some clothing to wear. After I was dressed, I went back to the clothes closet to get some oil to anoint my head but I remembered that the bottle was empty. I had made a mental note to put some oil in the bottle but I never did. Then I saw something amazing had taken place. I stood there in complete amazement. The oil bottle was a quarter full. I stood there gazing at this oil bottle. I did not want to touch it. I just wanted to look at it. How did this oil get into the bottle I asked myself? I know I did not put it there. Maybe Nancy, my wife, did. So I asked Nancy if she put any oil in the bottle and her response was no. So how did this oil get into the bottle? I am absolutely positive without a shadow of doubt the oil bottle was empty. I know for sure I never put any oil in the bottle. So where did it come from and when was this oil put into this bottle? I know this was a miracle from God that He put the oil into the bottle. Like the woman in the multiplying oil, God completely created some oil out of nothing and put it into the bottle. That Sunday morning God worked a miracle of creation. I called Nancy into the room and we both stood there and watched the bottle of oil. This was a very notable miracle that would later give rise to many more.

My comments at the time were that I believed this miracle was a sign that God would fulfill His promises to me. He promised that He would give me many more miracles and manifestations. Now I am looking for a manifestation of the gifts of the spirit. This was truly a sign for many miracles happened shortly thereafter.

QUESTIONS FOR GROUP DISCUSSION:

1. What role did faith and obedience play in this miracle?
2. Should we always seek God first in all things?
3. Constrast with Psalm 37:25.

CHAPTER

Face to Face

So the Lord spoke to Moses face to face,
as a man speaks to his friend.
Exodus 33:11

Moses was a great prophet and deliverer of God's people out of bondage in Egypt. In Exodus 32 we see Israel break the covenant with God it had previously made. Moses had ascended to the top of the mountain to talk and meet with God. The people saw that Moses delayed in coming down from the mountain so they gathered themselves together unto Aaron the priest. The people said to Aaron, "Up, make us gods to worship as for Moses we do not know what happened to him." Aaron then instructed them to break off the golden earrings which were in the ears of the people and bring them to him. The people broke off all the earrings, and brought them to Aaron. Aaron then made the people a molten calf, and the people said, "These be the gods, O Israel." Aaron then built an altar before the molten calf and made a proclamation. He declared that tomorrow would be a feast to the Lord. Early the next day the people rose up early and offered burnt offerings and peace offerings. Then the people sat down to eat and to drink and rose up to play. They engaged in idolatrous behavior which included whoredoms, sport, fornication, and laughter. Almost all Israel dipped low in sin and moral depravity during Moses' absence.

God told Moses to get down from the mountain for the people had corrupted themselves. God told Moses what the people had done. Then God told Moses to let Him alone so that He may consume them. It was God's intention to make Moses a great nation. Moses said to the Lord that the Egyptians would say that God saved His people only to consume them. Moses then asked the Lord God to turn from His fierce wrath and repent of this evil against His people. Then Moses reminded God of Abraham, Isaac, and Israel by which He swore to multiply their seed as the stars of heaven. Moses further stated that God had promised to give the land to their seed as an inheritance forever. God changed His mind of the evil which He thought to do against Israel.

Moses and Joshua then left the mount with the tablets and heard the noise of the people. Joshua said to Moses, "this is the shout of war in the camp." Moses replied, "This is not a shout of war, but of them that sing." As Moses and Joshua came close to the camp they saw the calf. They also witnessed the dancing and all the idolatrous activities. This made Moses very angry. Moses cast the tablets out of his hands at the base of the mountain and broke them. Moses took the molten calf, ground it to powder, then strewed it upon the water and made the children of Israel to drink it. Moses asked Aaron, "What did the people do to you that you have brought so great a sin upon them?" Aaron immediately blamed the people saying, "They are set on mischief." Aaron explained to Moses that the people wanted him to make them gods. When Moses saw that the people were naked, he stood in the gate of the camp. Moses then said, "Who is on the Lord's side?

Let them come to me." All the sons of Levi came to him. Moses told them to put every man his sword by his side, and go in and out of the gate and slay their brothers, companions and neighbors. According to Moses about three thousand men died by the Levites. The next day Moses told the people, "Ye have sinned a great sin" and that he would make an atonement for their sins. Moses told God that the people had sinned a great sin, but he knew He could forgive their sins. Moses said if you don't forgive them, then blot me out of thy book. God's response to Moses was "Whosoever hath sinned against me, him will I blot out of my book." God told Moses to go and lead the people to the place He had told him. God further said He would send an angel before them and He would visit their sins upon them. Then God punished the people because of the molten calf which Aaron had made.

In Exodus 33 God first tells Moses to depart and go to the land He swore unto his forefathers. He told him He would send an angel before him and He would drive out all the enemies of Israel. He would bring them to a land flowing with milk and honey. This was a figurative term meaning all the goodness of God. God said He would not go up in the midst of them because they were stiffnecked. God warned He might consume them in the way. When the people heard these words they mourned. Then He said, "put off the ornaments from thee that I may know what I will do with you." Then the children of Israel stripped themselves of their ornaments at the base of Mount Horeb. Moses took the tabernacle and pitched it without the camp far from the camp and called it the tabernacle of the congregation. Every one that sought the Lord went unto the tabernacle of the congregation outside of the camp. Then one of the most incredible supernatural events took place for all of Israel to see. Moses went into the tabernacle, and all the people rose up and stood every man in his tent door. They looked until Moses had gone into the tabernacle. As Moses entered into the tabernacle, the cloudy pillar descended. The cloudy pillar stood at the door of the tabernacle and God talked with Moses. God came down to talk with Moses and persuade the people that Moses was the deliverer. This was very much a normal conversation held by God and Moses as a friend would speak to another friend. The children of Israel could hear God and Moses conversing back and forth between themselves. All the children of Israel saw the cloudy pillar stand at the tabernacle door. Then all the people rose and worshipped in their tent door.

Probably one of the most intriguing things in the entire Bible took place. God the father, the God of the entire universe spoke with Moses face to face. God spoke as a man speaks to his friend. Then Moses turned again into the camp but Joshua did not depart from the tabernacle.

Joshua was an upclose witness of the fact that God spoke with Moses face to face. Without a shadow of a doubt Joshua heard the entire conversation between God and Moses.

I have had many face to face encounters with God in my ministry, but probably the one that had the most profound impression upon me took place in October 1992. In June 1992 I met Reverend Tim Colisino. I had known Reverend Colisino for a number of years so we conversed for a while.

We discussed the Holy Ghost and the need to renew the teachings of this great doctrine. Many churches, pastors and ministries had forgotten the importance of Pentecost. We discussed getting together again and maybe joining ministries to preach about the Holy Ghost. He invited me to preach at his church. I accepted to come and preach in October.

It was a sunny October Sunday morning. Nancy, Kirsten and Kris Adam accompanied me. We had a glorious song service. I felt the personal presence of the Holy Ghost. I preached the message and gave an invitation to Christ then something truly incredible happened. As I was standing there, the Holy Ghost raised both my hands over my head. I tried to put them down but I could not. I could feel a hand on my right arm and on my left arm. These hands held up both my arms for about twenty minutes as I spoke in tongues. It appeared as if God had opened up the heavens because of the supernatural. The nine gifts of the spirit was operating and I prophesied. This was a great service as God fell upon the entire congregation.

Reverend Colisino invited me back two weeks later in October to bring the message. Again my family accompanied me to the church. We had another glorious song service and I could feel the presence of the Holy Ghost. As Reverend Colisino called me up to the pulpit to preach the congregation was still singing. I walked up to the pulpit and stood behind it looking at the congregation. Then I saw this incredible sight. It was the Holy Ghost. He was standing at the rear of the church in between the pews on the right side. He was about six feet tall with hair to his shoulders. He was wearing a long white robe which seemed to sparkle. My eyes were totally fixed on Him at this time. I did not move a muscle I just stared at Him the entire time. Then He started to move up the aisle toward me. As He came closer I was able to see face to face that He was truly God. I was looking at God face to face as He was about ten feet away from me. Then He said, "Have all the people come to the altar." I told all the congregation to come to the altar. They all came to the altar for prayer. The Holy Ghost then came and stood about one foot away from me. I was now looking at God, the Holy Ghost face to face. I could see perfectly that He was God and yet a man that stood in front of me. After about two minutes of looking at God face to face one of the most incredible things happened. God moved closer and closer to me until he walked directly into my body. God literally walked straight into my body, and I felt this very intense heat. This heat covered my entire body and my insides felt like fire. Then something very unusual took place in my body. My spirit was removed and the Holy Ghost was totally directing my body and speech. This was the most incredible feeling I have ever experienced. I went around laying hands on people and many were instantly healed. Some spoke in different tongues and some said they felt great power resonate through their bodies. One supernatural thing after another took place that Sunday morning. The service ended with miracles of various kinds. That October Sunday morning at East Run Pentecostal Ministry I came face to face with God.

Questions for Group Discussion:

1. Discuss the realities of meeting God face to face.

2. Does God appear to everyone?
3. Discuss Moses' face to face encounters with God.

Epilogue

So the Lord spoke to Moses face to face,
as a man speaks to his friend.
Exodus 33:11

Since my last supernatural encounter at East Run Pentecostal Church mentioned in chapter 25, the supernatural has been a constant occurrence. In June of 2000 I was startled and amazed. I was led by the Holy Ghost to start a ministry in McKeesport, Pennsylvania. I was praying at Morris Park in Fairmont, West Virginia, a place where I would often go to pray, and I heard the voice of the Holy Ghost say to me, "you need to surrender." My response was "I am already totally surrendered to you Lord God." The Holy Spirit said to me, "No, you are not. There are some things you still need to surrender." My response was, "Yes Lord." I pondered what it was that I had not surrendered to Him that night.

In my final prayer of the evening I heard the Holy Ghost say, "Take a white handkerchief to the park tomorrow when you pray." The next day I went to Morris Park to pray and after a short time in prayer I heard the Holy Ghost say, "It's time for you to surrender. Take the handkerchief that's in your right hand and wave it over your head and repeat over and over again I surrender, I surrender all." So, I took the handkerchief and raised it above my head and repeated the words I was given by the Holy Ghost, "I surrender, I surrender all" over and over again until I was told to stop. The Holy Spirit said, "From today on you will have no aspirations of success and no thoughts or desires to do anything unless you are told by God." So from that day on my life was a blank slate for the Holy Ghost to write on.

I received a call from my sister, Reverend Dorothy Reeves, to come preach a series of meetings at her church in McKeesport, Pennsylvania. I accepted the invitation and after the meetings were over I was asked to preach for Reverends John and Naomi Green who had converted a large house into a church. In this series of meeting there were great miracles, signs, wonders and many supernatural occurrences. One in particular was that of an elderly woman that could not eat solid food. She had not been able to eat solid food for 10 years. This night she came forward and asked me to pray that she would be able to eat solid food again. I asked her if she believed that Jesus would heal her and told her that from that night on she would be able to eat solid food. She responded, "I know Jesus is going to heal me!" I anointed her head with oil and prayed that she would be able to eat solid food tonight. She asked, "If I stop and buy some chicken tonight I'll be able to eat it?" My response was, "Yes you can!"

The following week during a Sunday night service this same elderly lady gave her testimony that after she left the service last Sunday night she bought some chicken at 11:00 pm and ate it that night. Since then she has eaten everything and has been perfectly fine. She thanked and praised God for all his goodness and mercy for her healing.

In the next couple of months I did a series of meetings in different churches in McKeesport and the surrounding vicinity. In this one particular meeting where I was ministering I met three women. We later became very good friends. I was invited to do some meetings in their home on Saturdays. The meetings started out with only five to ten people and grew to fifty then to a hundred. These were great times of praising and worshipping with great manifestations from God. I continued to hold meetings in their home for one year. Often times the services started at 7:00 p.m. and lasted to 7:00 a.m. the next day. People would come and go all night. Some of the most spectacular moves of the Holy Ghost were witnessed. One of the marvelous things was the healing of a young man who had liver cancer. He heard about the meetings from a friend who recommended that he go see what was truly happening there. He came with his aunt and he told me that he had liver cancer. I asked him if he believed God would heal him and he said, "Yes, I do." I laid hands on him and prayed a short prayer and told him he was healed. He then began to shake and fell backward to the floor. He lay there for an hour. After he woke up he said he felt a hot heat start at the top of his head and went to his feet. He left that night knowing that he was healed and the next week he returned and gave his testimony that the doctors had declared that he was completely cancer free and there was not a single trace of it in his body.

We continued week after week with great manifestations of God. One in particular took place after the service ended about 4:00 a.m. and about ten people were sitting around discussing the great things we had witnessed. Then out of nowhere a strong wind started to blow on all of us. We stopped talking. The wind stopped blowing and when we started talking again the wind started blowing again. This happened all morning until we left and went home. This started one of the greatest moves of the Holy Ghost we had ever seen with great miracles, signs and wonders that went beyond all that we had seen before.

In June of 2000 I started the Elisha Ministry Church and it now has expanded to a much larger ministry which now includes the prophetic with even greater signs, wonders, miracles and supernatural manifestations of the Holy Ghost to this current day.

Additional copies of *The Good Hand of God* and other titles
from Dawn Treader Publications are available
through your local bookstore, online at Amazon.com
and other vendors, or directly from the Publisher.

The author may be reached by contacting the Publisher
or online at www.morningstarandcompany.org

Dawn Treader Publications
He who treads the dawn is the Bright and Shining Morning Star™

A Ministry of Morning Star And Company, Inc.
Post Office Box 24405
Lyndhurst, OH 44124

Colophon

Set in Book Antiqua and Bell Gothic
Printed and Bound in the United States of America

Book Layout and Design by KAR at Studio Downstairs
Cover art is a portion from *The Creation of Adam* by Michelangelo
(from the Sistine Chapel's ceiling, painted c. 1511–1512)
that depicts a narrative from the Biblical Book of Genesis
in which God breathes life into Adam, the first man.

www.ingramcontent.com/pod-product-compliance
Lightning Source LLC
LaVergne TN
LVHW041623070426
835507LV00008B/419